Appreciation

At one point we stood to lose a lot of potential business, and your Vaastu advice really saved the day. We could not have come this far without your Vaastu support.

R.L. Agarwal
Director
Darcl Logistic Limited

I am writing to appreciate your friendly cooperation and great vaastu advice. Thank you for your excellent services. Your professionalism and positive attitude is greatly appreciated.

Avdhesh Kumar Goel
Joint Managing Director
Earth Infrastructure Ltd.

We wouldn't have come across such a long way emphatically without your support. Vaastu has definite impact on business & life if guided in the right direction and your guidance has proved to be a lighthouse for our business.

Neeraj Aggarwal
Director
Synergy Waste Management (P) Ltd.

Accept my heartfelt gratitude in helping me achieve my goals and ambitions. I recommend your services to all who wish to experience the rewards of 100% result oriented customized vaastu solutions with fullest faith.

Ravindra Gautam
Managing Director
Aquarius Mediaa (P) Limited

I feel indebted to you for persuading me to change my old office set up at Jangpura and brought me to new office at Bengali Market which was built under your guidance. I really enjoy and cherish my work at my new place.

Ajay Bansal
Additional Advocate General, Punjab
Supreme Court of India

VAASTU

Vedic Architectural Wisdom for Modern Buildings

N
NW
NE
W
E
SW
SE
S

VAASTU

Vedic Architectural Wisdom for Modern Buildings

Naresh Singal

Bharat Singal

STERLING PUBLISHERS (P) LTD.
Regd. Office: A1/256 Safdarjung Enclave, New Delhi-110029.
Cin: U22110DL1964PTC211907
Mobile: +91 82877 98380/+91 120-6251823
e-mail: mail@sterlingpublishers.in
www.sterlingpublishers.in

Vaastu: Vedic Architectural Wisdom for Modern Buildings
Originally published as:
Vaastu for Harmony in 2013
© 2015, Naresh Singal & Bharat Singal
ISBN 978 81 207 9654 6
First Edition 2015
Reprint 2019, 2021

Cover designed by
Abhimanyu Sinha

Printed in India

Printed and Published by Sterling Publishers Pvt. Ltd.,
Plot No. 13, Ecotech-III, Greater Noida-201306, U P, India

OM

I dedicate this book to
my loving parents
who brought me into this world and
gave an opportunity to serve humanity!

Naresh Singal

Preface

"Why don't you write a book on Vaastu?" I have been frequently asked this question by my valued clients, students, as well as a majority of those who have been attending my free vaastu workshops.

They would advise me, "Your straightforward and practical approach has drawn us to Vaastu, and so we want you to put it all in a book, which will be our general guide on the subject."

I could obviously not ignore such a genuine request of my clients, students and followers. Thus the long awaited book is right in your hands now. I am most pleased to present this humble work to you.

Ever since I was initiated in this divine discipline by my revered mentor late Dr. Dronam Raju Poornachandra Rao, I cherished a desire to pass on the rare knowledge imparted to me by my illustrious *Gurudev*, which has proved authentic through years of successful practice.

Even I went through several stores, flooded with loads of books on the subject, I failed to find a 'down to earth' and practical book on Vaastu, truly addressed to the need of a layman.

Many such books deal in jargon, making this subject dry and impracticable to a layman.

Blessings of my great Guru and years of thorough study and research on my part helped me to dive deep into the vast ocean of knowledge and come out with some rare gems. I believe, these gems as revealed through this book, will usher health, harmony and happiness into your life. The growing number of my students, clients and followers is ample evidence of my sincere efforts in this discipline.

Needless to say, there do exist several genuine consultants in this field, but conspicuous with their presence are also a few 'so called Vaastu consultants' who misguide people with their little and shallow knowledge. One has to be wary of such fakes.

I remember the golden words-

"There are three categories of people:

1: Those who know not and do not know that they don't know; they are fools.

2: Those who know not and know that they don't know; they are teachable, teach them.

3: Those who know and know that they know; they are wise, follow them."

It is you readers who has the right to decide in which category you want to put me in. After going through this book you can judge it better. I think I know my job well and can guide you through your vaastu problems, thus enabling you to enjoy a life full of prosperity, peace and harmony.

I hope you find my humble effort worthwhile. I will appreciate your honest opinion and suggestions, if any.

Naresh Singal
Bharat Singal

Contents

Section-C
Vaastu in Practice

Introduction

Vaastoshpatey pratijanihyasmaan swavesho anmivo bhava naha,
Yatvemahi prati tanno jushsav sham no bhav dwipadey sham chatushpadey.

We worship and hail to thee and perform sacrificial act, O' Vaastudeva; the lord of land for living! May you protect us from disease and untimely sorrow and grant us peace by safeguarding our dear ones and our animal-treasure.

- Rigveda

The above Vedic verse (*mantra*) is a prayer to the vaastu lord for protection and peace. And peace is the greatest need of the modern man.

Peace leads to harmony, and harmony alone ensures an all round progress. This book promises peace and harmony in the lives of the readers who approach it sincerely.

The book is divided into three sections namely:

A: Understanding Vaastu, B: The Roots or Basis of Vaastu, and C: Vaastu in Practice

Section-A carries seven chapters. Chapter 1: *What is Vaastu?* traces the origin of the word 'vaastu' and elucidates the meaning of its related terms. It explains how this ancient science differs from the modern day architecture. It critically appreciates the role of vaastu in rise and fall of civilisations. The reader will get acquainted with the names of sages and teachers who made significant contributions to the development of vaastu. This chapter seeks to represent vaastu in the right perspective.

The second chapter, *The Scientific Basis of Vaastu* explores, as the title implies, the scientific basis of this ancient branch of knowledge.

The third chapter titled, *Vaastu Remedies without Demolition* clarifies that demolishing an existing structure is not the only remedy for vaastu defects which can be rectified by many other measures.

The fourth chapter *Vaastu and Astrology* elaborately examines the relationship between vaastu and astrology. But a million dollar question is: "how to know that a premises is under some vaastu defect? " which is logically answered in the fifth chapter titled - *Is Your Premises Under Vaastu Defect?*

Some sceptics question the relevance of vaastu to the modern life. The sixth chapter titled *Relevance and Benefits of Vaastu* deals with this aspect. The last chapter of this section carries some frequently asked questions about vaastu and their answers.

Section-B titled - *The Roots or Basis of Vaastu* contains seven chapters. Chapter One, *Vaastu Purush and Mandalas* explains the concept of Vaastu Purush, its legend and relevance to a plot of land.

Chapter Two is titled *Vaastu and Elements* and elaborates the five elements considered essential to vaastu.

The role of the natural forces or energies in vaastu is described in the third chapter titled, *Vaastu and Natural Forces.* It deals with the seven types of energies, viz. Celestial Energy, Gravitational Energy, Magnetic Energy, Solar Energy, Ultraviolet Energy, Infrared Energy and Subtle Energies.

The importance of directions in vaastu is detailed within the fourth chapter *Vaastu and Directions.*

The type and nature of soil of a place is of prime importance in vaastu and needs to be considered while selecting a plot of land for construction. Different types of land and their use are enumerated in chapter five - *Vaastu and Plot of Land.*

Not all plots are square or rectangular. One comes across different shapes of plots. Some are symmetrical while others are not. Vaastu results for different shapes of plots are given in the sixth chapter *Shapes of Plots and Vaastu.*

The corners of a plot of land are crucial in vaastu as these are junctions of two different directions. The last chapter of this section *Plots with Extended and Torn Corners* deals with this important aspect.

Section-C of this book is titled *Vaastu in Practice* and contains 27 chapters. Chapter one *Important Vaastu Mahuratas* recounts some important Mahuratas (auspicious hours) related to purchasing a plot and constructing a building on it. The second chapter, *Planning According to Directions* discusses how directions should be kept in mind while planning the map of a house.

Chapter three of this section is about auspicious symbols and tools in vaastu, their implications and uses. The areas and plots adjoining the plot of one's interest need some probing before it is being bought as these have a bearing on the auspiciousness of the land. This aspect is examined in chapter four titled- *Importance of Adjoining Plots.*

Vaastu principles and remedial measures related to various parts of a house from the main entrance to a veranda are described separately in chapters five to twenty eight, respectively titled *The Main Entrance, The Brahmasthan, Basement, Bathroom, Bedrooms, Boring for Water, Children's Room, Dining Room, Drawing Room, Electric Meter and Equipment, Garage, Guard Room, Guest Room, Jumble Room, Kitchen, Overhead Water Tank, Pet Animals, Prayer Room, Servant's Room, Staircase, Storeroom, Studyroom, Toilet, Veranda.*

Admitting that you cannot take the place of an experienced vaastu consultant just by reading a couple of books, this book aims at enriching your knowledge on the subject and equip you with some practical tips which you can apply to your benefit and prosper.

I hope you will like this book and enjoy reading it.

Naresh Singal

mail@vaastunaresh.com

Understanding Vaastu

STOP
Vaastu

What is Vaastu?

Nature inspires human beings to be inquisitive about its mysteries. Once inspired, the inquisitive and deep thinking minds impel it to reveal its secrets.

Western scientists are able to decipher only the physical nature of things, whereas the great Indian *Rishis* and *Maharishis* (spiritual scientists) could transcend the physical and grab some rare gems.

Vaastu is one such gem which has been polished over centuries by the wise, many sages and *acharyas* (teachers).

How the word vaastu originated?

The word vaastu is derived from the Sanskrit word *Vaas*, meaning a residence or a place of residence. As the Vaastu Purush legend goes (see the next section), the devtas (gods) on insisted by Lord Brahma got hold of the giant demon, each devta holding a particular part of the demon and pinning him down on earth with his face down.

Lord Brahma was happy and appreciated this brave act of the devtas and blessed them. As a reward, he granted them residence or *vaas* in the respective parts of the demon. Hence the word *vaastu*.

The word vaastu and related terms

The word *vaastu* means a site for a building or a building or a structure. In this context, generally, one comes across three distinctive terms viz. *Vaastu Kala, Vaastu Vigyan* and *Vaastu Shastra,* which merit to be clearly defined.

We all know that architecture is an art as well as a science. The art part is concerned with the aesthetic sense, which takes care of the outer beauty and novelty of a structure, and the related term is *Vaastu-Kala.* This in general also stands for architecture.

As for the science part, it concerns the mechanical strength, gravitational balance, safety from natural calamities, etc. The term used in this context is *Vaastu-Vigyan.* This also, in general, stands for architecture.

Vaastu Shastra refers to the treatises and scriptures which contain the original information on the subject.

How vaastu differs from modern architecture?

The modern architecture is restricted to the above mentioned factors but the ancient Indian architecture, known generally as *vaastu* (in short for Vaastu Kala or Vaastu Vigyan), also takes care of some more subtle and unseen influences such as cosmic energy, directional effects, elemental effects, earth's magnetic field, gravitation, magnetic and light energy from the sun (solar energy), and the planetary effects.

Vaastu behind rise and fall of civilisations

In many archaeological remains of ancient civilisations we find indications of or absence of vaastu based designs and planning. Thus, a detailed joint study by historians and vaastu experts can reveal some astonishing facts that might have caused the rise and fall of those civilisations.

There are legends about the fall of certain kingdoms merely due to serious vaastu defects in palaces and forts.

Vaastu based planning of the pink city of Jaipur in Rajasthan is a living example of the positive effect of vaastu. The credit of Jaipur's golden and prosperous past as well as its glorious present is unerringly attributed to vaastu.

There was a serious vaastu defect in the palace of the king of Nepal which led to the tragic and bloody end of the kingdom.

Is vaastu meant for people of one faith only?

India is a land of gods embracing a rich culture based on Vedas, Puranas and Upanishads. The knowledge of vaastu also has been passed on through these scriptures. Some people doubt whether vaastu is to be followed only by those who have faith in these scriptures. No, vaastu is like any other science and its use is not limited to any one faith or religion. In fact, vaastu has nothing to do with religion. Although claiming an Indian origin, it may be used by people of all religions and faiths.

Faith does wonder!

Why do we regard certain plants like Peepal, Ashoka, and Tulsi as sacred and worship these? Well, there must have been reasons our wise ancient Rishis knew well. So, if we give up scepticism and have faith then only we can benefit. The same holds good for the vaastu principles. Why condemn this ancient sacred science vis-à-vis the very limited knowledge the modern western science has to offer?

Many renowned vaastu consultants of have many authentic case histories where people have definitely benefited from expert advice and guidance.

Is vaastu a recent development?

The science of vaastu is as old as the vedas, the most ancient Hindu scriptures, considered the original source of all knowledge. Some people may argue: why vaastu knowledge was not used during the Vedic Kaal (the age of vedas)? A careful study reveals that during the vedic period vaastu principles were followed. Vaastu like any other art or science has gradually developed to its present state. Apart from the vedas the other scriptures like *Matsya Puraan, Varaha Puraan, Brahma Vaivarta Puraan, Skand Puraan, Aagneya Puraan, Devi Bhagvat Puraan, Kalki Puraan, Bhavishotar Puraan* and *Vishnu Dharmotar Puraan* also contain information about this science.

The great acharyas (teachers) of vaastu

Besides, vaastu references are found in ancient literature like Baalmiki's *Ramayan* and *Mahabharata*. These treatises also mention the names of 18 great acharyas of this great science. These acharyas were: Mrig, Aarya, Vashishtha, Vishwakarma, Maya, Naarad, Naganjit, Vishalaksh, Purandar, Brahma, Kumar, Nandish, Shounak, Garg, Vaasudev, Anirudh, Shukra and Brihaspati.

According to the *Aagneya Puraan* there were 25 vaastu acharyas whereas the *Maansagar* treatise mentions 32. *Brahmsamhita* also mentions the names of Bhaskar and Manu besides the above 18.

The Kashyap Shilp claims Maharishi Kashyap to be the pioneering acharya of vaastu shastra.

In fact, there is no precise account of the treatises related to vaastu originally produced and those existing today. Some important treatises were unfortunately destroyed by the unscrupulous foreign invaders.

Can vaastu principles change our destiny?

As professed *"Bhagya se adhik or samay se pehley kuchch nahi milta"*, which means you get nothing beyond your luck and before the time is ripe.

People normally believe that merely a visit by a vaastu consultant to their premises will shower prosperity and abundance on them, which is absolutely unrealistic. Truly the vaastu principles may help remove the obstacles, but you get only that amount of health, happiness and prosperity which destiny has allocated for you.

So a vaastu practitioner with his expertise and guidance only helps you clear whatever impedes your luck.

This humble book proposes to instruct and enlighten you about this great science and thus enabling you to enjoy a life of contentment.

Do not confuse vaastu with feng shui

It is confounding that some writers have mixed the two different sciences.

Some books on vaastu give feng shui methods without distinction and confuse the common people. The two sciences are quite apart.

Scientific Basis of Vaastu

The modern man is inquisitive and discards ideas which defy logic. Some doubt efficacy of vaastu. They question scientific validity of vaastu and ask : is it not merely an ancient belief system?

Have you ever speculated the finite nature of science? The scientific knowledge and methods at a particular time in history have certain limits and operate only on the physical plane. All phenomena beyond such boundaries are considered supernatural and generally not believed by scientists. With continuing developments and opening of human mind the boundaries of science keep expanding all the time.

There should be no doubt that vaastu has a scientific basis. This is in fact is an ancient science as well as an art. Some of the basis of vaastu can be comprehended as per the present state of science but the rest is still beyond its scope. Whether or not we understand all the concepts and principles of vaastu they continue to operate and affect our lives.

There are lots of things which the present day science cannot explain convincingly. On what logic are acupuncture and acupressure based? But so many people who show faith get cured of various ailments.

Some people unnecessarily argue when they are advised to sleep with their head towards south. They question its scientific basis and shrug it off as mere superstition. In fact, our body is a magnet with the head as north pole and the feet as south pole. When we sleep with our head (north pole) towards the earth's south pole there is magnetic attraction between opposite poles and we enjoy a sound and relaxing sleep.

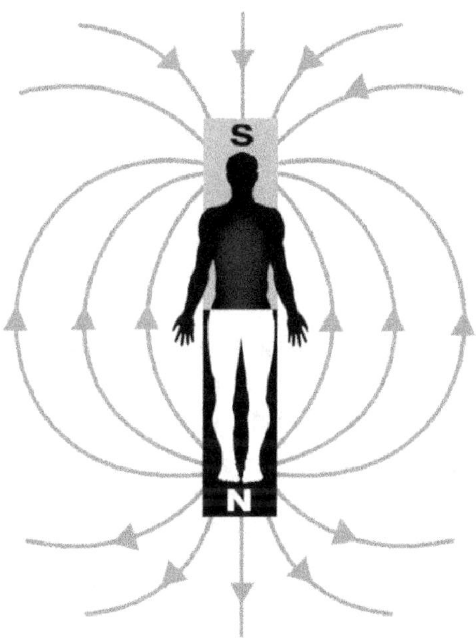

If one is advised to sit facing north for important discussions the same magnetic effects are under consideration. The magnetic force from north is conducive to arriving at some positive conclusion during a discussion.

As advised by vaastu, everyone likes to go for an east facing house or commercial premises which cannot be brushed off as mere superstition as it is based on the fact that the sun's rays coming from east contain ultraviolet rays which are rich in Vitamins A, D and a lot of energy, and so rejuvenate our body and mind.

Vaastu science advises us to locate the kitchen in the southeast corner, because in that part the ultraviolet rays of the sun not only give germ-free fresh air but positively impact the housewife as well.

The wisdom of vaastu requires that the walls on the north and east sides should be light, thin and low as compared to those on the south and west sides. This is because the morning rays of the sun being rich in ultraviolet rays are good and should enter the premises unhindered. Thinner and lower walls on these sides will facilitate free and ample incoming of these healthy rays.

As the day advances the sun's rays become rich in infrared content which is harmful to our health, so these harmful rays should be blocked with thicker and higher walls on south and west sides.

Scientists have recognised the effects of the sun and the moon and their related phenomena on change of seasons, earth quakes and other atmospheric effects.

During the periods when the sun and the moon fall in line facing each other or come together, the gravitational forces affect onset of tides and cyclones.

So it is clear that the great science of vaastu has a solid scientific basis and if it is followed with faith it can transform our lives for good.

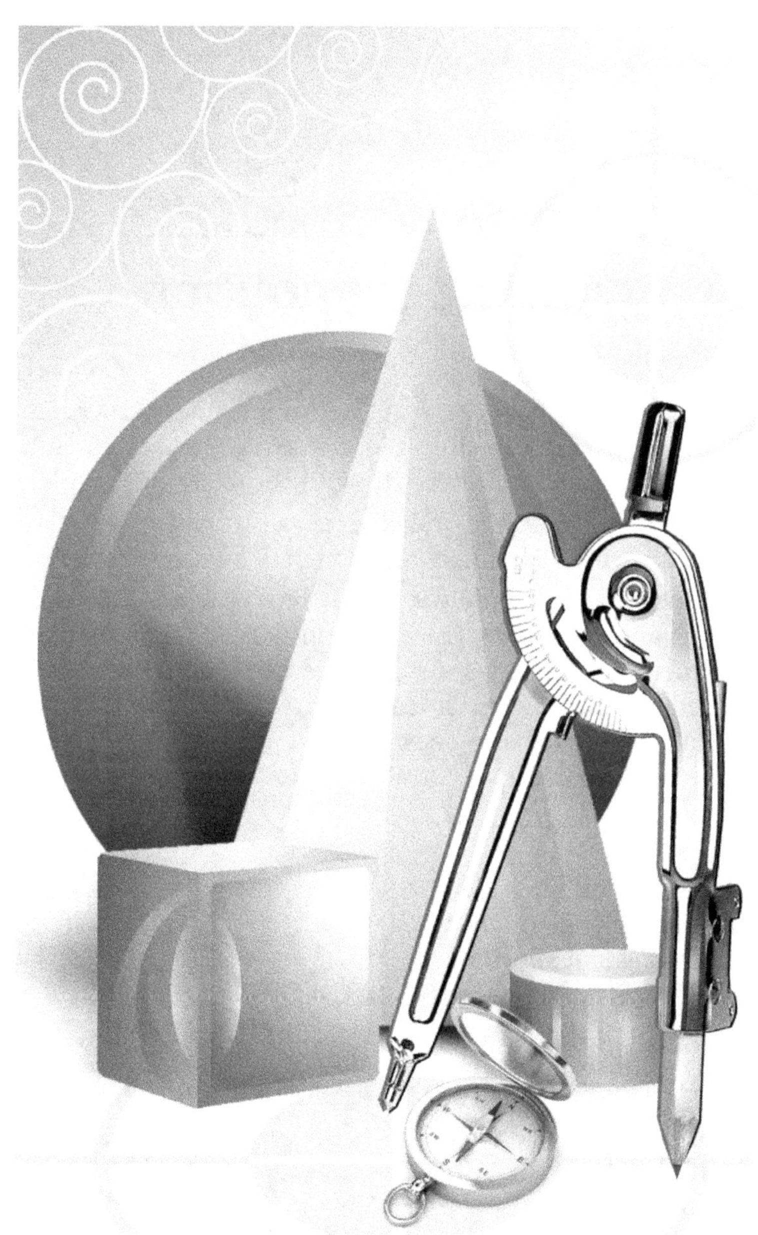

Vaastu Remedies without Demolition

I t is wrongly believed that one can benefit from vaastu only by demolishing the defective structures and rebuilding them in conformity with the vaastu principles.

Only quackish and mercenary vaastu consultants are responsible for such misrepresentation of this sacred science.

These days, people are much more aware than ever before and take extra care to construct new houses or commercial buildings in accordance with the vaastu principles. But when it comes to already constructed buildings which have vaastu *doshas* (defects) people are sometimes misled.

Many people these days are living in rented houses or state provided accommodation. So when some vaastu consultant advises them to demolish certain defective parts and rebuild the same as instructed by them, people are utterly confounded. Their inability to follow the consultant's advice leads people to misconceptions about the science of vaastu.

A genuine and competent vaastu consultant knows that demolition is not the only remedy. A lot can be done without demolition to partly or fully reduce the negative effects of vaastu defects.

By judicious rearrangements of interiors and use of certain methods such as mirrors, chimes, lighting, plants, pyramids, *yantras-mantras*, gemstones, vaastu crystals, *rudraksha* beads, vaastu energy plate, landscaping, auspicious trees, an expert vaastu consultant can help people in getting peace and prosperity and minimise the negative effects of vaastu defects.

The above mentioned methods are described below:

1. **Mirrors:** If there is a vaastu defect (*dosha*) in the northeast direction then fixing a mirror there can alleviate the defect. A mirror helps in enlarging any restricted or tight area and thus covers any defect.

   A mirror fitted at a jeweller's shop, restaurant and hotel also enhances the ambience besides adding to the beauty of the place in addition to covering any defect.

   In a south facing premises, or that with torn corners and defective kitchen or toilet, a mirror can eliminate the defects.

2. **Wind chimes:** Many types of wind chimes are available nowadays. By hanging chimes of different melodies one can harmonise the vibrations of negative areas in a building.

3. **Lighting:** A house with torn corners can be cured of vaastu defects by utilising lights of various colours. The main entrance of a house must be well-lit. Any room in the north-west corner must be kept well-lit and clean.

4. **Plants:** By keeping potted plants at certain places one can reduce or eliminate vaastu defects. If there is a staircase facing the main entrance, potted plants should be placed along the stairs. To render auspiciousness to the main entrance it should be flanked by potted plants.

5. **Vaastu pyramids:** The pyramids are located in many parts of the world. Pyramid is a huge structure made of stones with slanting triangular sides pointing upwards.

   The name pyramid derives from 'Pyra' which stands for fire, and 'mid' meaning the middle. There is something mysterious about the pyramids and the name suggests some source of positive force existing in the middle part of these structures. This will become clearer after you learn that a Frenchman named Bovis once entered the chamber located at the middle of the Great Pyramid at Giza. He was amazed to see that some dead animals lying there had not deteriorated.

   Small replicas of pyramids are available and these can fill the relevant areas with positive energy thereby reducing the negative effects of vaastu related defects.

6. **Yantras:** Yantras are some specific figures or squares with some numbers inscribed with a sharp object on a piece of some metal like copper or silver or written with some specific ink on some sacred leaf.

   A yantra is to be made at some auspicious time and then energised by certain ritual or worship. A properly made and energised yantra is then kept in the pocket or tied on the body of the person needing certain remedy. For curing vaastu defects a relevant yantra can be fixed at a place where a defect exists.

   There are many types of yantras and each has some specific purpose to serve. There are nine yantras which correspond to each of the nine planets. A yantra of the relevant planet in whose direction the vaastu dosha exists can be fixed there in order to overcome the dosha.

Sooriya Yantra (yantra for the Sun):

6	1	8
7	5	3
2	9	4

Chandra Yantra (yantra for the Moon):

7	2	9
8	6	4
3	10	5

Yantra for Mars: This yantra is inscribed on a copper plate.

8	3	10
9	7	5
4	11	6

Yantra for Mercury: This yantra is inscribed on a silver plate.

9	4	11
10	8	6
5	12	7

Yantra for Jupiter: This yantra is inscribed on a gold or copper plate.

10	5	12
11	9	7
6	13	8

Yantra for Venus: This yantra is inscribed on a copper plate.

11	6	13
12	10	8
7	14	9

Yantra for Saturn: This yantra is inscribed on an iron, or lead plate.

12	7	14
13	11	9
8	15	10

Yantra for Rahu: This yantra is inscribed on a silver plate.

13	8	15
14	12	10
9	16	11

Yantra for Ketu: This yantra is inscribed on an iron or lead plate.

14	9	16
15	13	11
10	17	12

Durga Yantra: This yantra is inscribed on a silver or copper plate. A very powerful yantra capable of removing many vaastu defects, it should be fixed on the main entrance.

7. Mantras: The following mantras can be used for recitation, for propitiating the relevant deity or planet or for energising the yantras.

Table A 3.1: Mantras for Deities and Planets

Planet/Deity	Mantra
Sun	*'Om Ghrini Sooriyaye Namaha'*
Moon	*'Om shraam shreem shrom saha chandrai namaha'*
Mars	*'Om kraam kreem krom saha bhomai namaha'*
Mercury	*'Om braam breem brom saha budhai namaha'*
Jupiter	*'Om brim brihespatye namaha'*
Venus	*'Om shum shukrai namaha'*
Saturn	*'Om shamm shaneshcharai namaha'*
Rahu	*'Om ram rahvey namaha'*
Ketu	*'Om kem ketvey namaha'*
Durga	*'Om namo bhagvati vastudevaye namaha'*

8. Gemstones: Natural gemstones are great source of energy. There are nine gemstones which are governed by each of the nine planets of *Vedic* astrology and these are called *navratans* literally meaning the nine gems. These are listed in the table below:

Table A 3.2: The *Navratans* or gems governed by nine planets

Governing Planet	Gemstone
Sun	Ruby
Moon	Pearl
Mars	Red Coral
Mercury	Emerald
Jupiter	Yellow Sapphire
Venus	Diamond
Saturn	Blue Sapphire
Rahu	Hessonite
Ketu	Cat's Eye

A relevant gemstone can be worn in a ring by the person suffering from afflictions from corresponding planet.

9. Vaastu crystals: Naturally occurring quartz crystals are a source of energy. Crystal pyramids are also available. The quartz crystals kept in the north-west corner of a room help in harmonising family relations. These are also good for health and success in financial matters.

Crystal pyramids give peace, harmony and prosperity by absorbing the negative energy of premises. The other use of a crystal is to hang it in that direction of a room where a vaastu dosha exists.

10. Rudraksha beads: Rudraksha beads are considered very sacred. Rosaries made of rudraksha beads are used for mantra recitation.

According to a Hindu mythological legend, Lord Shiva used his weapon *aaghor* to destroy the demon called *Tripurasur*.

Due to the nature of the weapon used, tears dropped from Lord Shiva's eyes and grew up as trees whose fruits are called *rudraksha*.

It is believed that Lord Shiva bestows his blessings upon anyone using rudraksha beads for worshipping.

The rudraksha beads are classified from one to sixteen faces (*mukh*). These beads come in many sizes and the smallest ones are considered more precious.

The table below describes the various types of rudraksha beads:

Table A 3.3: Different types of *Rudraksha* beads and their benefits

No. Of faces (*mukh*)	Governing Deity	Lord Planet	Benefits of wearing
One	Lord Shiva	Sun	Gives comforts in life.
Two	Lord Shiva and Parvati	Moon	Improves concentration, gives contentment and success in spiritual pursuits.
Three	Agni	Mars	Gives wealth and success in education.
Four	Lord Brahma	Mercury	Cures stammering, gives success in study of mathematics, astrology and research. It is also believed to give progeny to barren women.
Five	Kalingan (Panch Brahma)	Jupiter	Gives peace, comforts, fame, wealth, knowledge and happiness.

Six	Kartikey or Ganesha	Venus	Gives success in education and cures hysteria, fainting, fits and many female diseases.
Seven	Saptrishis	Saturn	Cures afflictions caused by the planet Saturn.
Eight	Goddess Bhagvati	Rahu	Gives long life, name and fame, success in education and good health.
Nine	Bhairon, Yam	Ketu	Helps in spiritual development and protects from evil-eye.
Ten	Lord Vishnu	All the nine planets	Protects the wearer from litigation, snake bite and imprisonment.
Eleven	Lord Indra	--	Brings luck when kept in a place of worship or cash box. Good for married couples and their progeny.
Twelve	Lord Vishnu	--	Blesses with progeny and a comfortable life. Also gives protection from thieves.
Thirteen	Lord Vishva Devas	--	Gives health, wealth and comforts.
Fourteen	Lord Shiva & Hanuman ji	--	Gives fearlessness, courage and freedom from diversity.
Gauri Shankar Rudraksha	Lord Shankar	--	Bestows blessings upon the worshipper.

11. Vaastu Energy Plate: Energy plate is a plastic plate approximately eight inches square and about half inch thick with the relevant symbol inscribed on its surface and an aluminium wire wrapped all around.

An energy plate with a Swastika symbol hung at the main entrance gives health and harmony to the residents of that house.

An energy plate with a symbol of female egg and male sperm hang in the bedroom of a married couple, on the wall towards the feet while sleeping, gives marital bliss and progeny.

12. Landscaping: Landscape means the scene or background or surroundings. By rearranging or beautifying the surroundings or landscaping we can rectify certain vaastu related defects of the premises.

One or more of the following suggestions can be incorporated for landscaping:

1. Constructing boundary walls on west, south-west and south directions. Boundary walls in these directions should be thicker and higher than those in east, north and north-east directions.

2. Increasing load on the south and south-west direction by making it heavier or increasing the level.

3. Creating slopes of the land towards north, east and north-east so that water flows towards these directions.

4. Growing aromatic and auspicious plants, herbs and trees in the west direction of the plot.

13. Auspicious Trees: The auspiciousness of the birth *nakshatra* (constellation) can be increased by planting an auspicious tree corresponding to that nakshatra as given in the table below:

Table A 3.4: Auspicious tree corresponding to the birth Nakshatra

S.No.	Birth Nakshatra	Auspicious Tree
1	*Ashvini*	*Kuchli*
2	*Bharni*	*Awali (Emblica offi.)*
3(A)	*Kritika* (The 1ˢᵗ quarter)	*Umber*
3(B)	*Kritika* (Remaining three quarters)	*Uwmber*
4	*Rohini*	*Jambhli (Syzygium cu.)*
5(A)	*Mrigshira* (First two quarters)	*Khair (Prosopis ciner.)*
5(B)	*Mrigshira* (Last two quarters)	*Khair (Prosopis ciner.)*
6	*Ardra*	*Krishngaru (Acquilaria)*
7(A)	*Punarvasu* (First three quarters)	*Velu (Dendro.Stricis)*
7(B)	*Punarvasu* (Fourth quarter)	*Velu (Dendro.Stricis)*
8	*Pushya*	*Pimpal (Ficus religiosa)*
9	*Ashlesha*	*Nagchafa (Mesua ferrea)*
10	*Magha*	*Vat (Ficus Bengalensis)*
11	*Purvaphalguni*	*Palas (Butea monosper)*
12(A)	*Uttaraphalguni* (First quarter)	*Dhayari (Buxus sempe.)*
12(B)	*Uttaraphalguni* (Last three quarters)	*Dhayari (Buxus sempe.)*
13	*Hasta*	*Jayi (Jasmin auriculata)*

14(A)	*Chitra* (First two quarters)	*Bel (Aegle marmelos)*
14(B)	*Chitra* (Last two quarters)	*Bel (Aegle marmelos)*
15	*Swati*	*Arjun (Termindia arj.)*
16(A)	*Vishakha* (First three quarters)	*Nagkeshar (Mesua fera)*
16(B)	*Vishakha* (Fourth quarter)	*Nagkeshar (Mesua fera)*
17	*Anuradha*	*Nagkeshar (Mesua fera)*
18	*Jyeshtha*	*Samber*
19	*Moola*	*Ral (Shorea robusta)*
20	*Purvashadha*	*Vet*
21(A)	*Uttarashadha* (First quarter)	*Phanas (Jackfruit Tree)*
21(B)	*Uttarashadha* (Last three quarters)	*Phanas (Jackfruit Tree)*
22	*Shravan*	*Rui (Gossypium arbo.)*
23(A)	*Dhanishtha* (First two quarters)	*Shami*
23(B)	*Dhanishtha* (Last two quarters)	*Shami*
24	*Shatabhisha*	*Shami*
25(A)	*Purvabhadrapad* (First three quarters)	*Kalamb*
25(B)	*Purvabhadrapad* (The last quarter)	*Amra (Mangifera ind.)*
26	*Uttarabhadrapad*	*Kadulimb (Azadiracta)*
27	*Revati*	*Moha (Madhuca lati.)*

Vaastu and Astrology

There is a very strong and vital link between vaastu and astrology. Notably, in this book when we talk about astrology we refer to the Hindu or vedic astrology. Why so? Are we biased? No, there is no such bias rather we are concerned with the depth and precision, which only vedic astrology can ensure.

Let us remind that vaastu and astrology both work for the comfort, security and prosperity of human beings.

A house may be shared by several members and each one of them has his or her unique luck or destiny. The destiny of a person is indicated by astrological factors like planets, constellation, and planetary periods (dashas), etc. All this can be inferred from the birth chart of that person.

On the other hand, vaastu is related to a plot of land or premises. Factors like plot shape, force of gravity, celestial rays, directions and adjoining conditions, etc., determine the effect on the lives of its occupants.

There are several instances where the owner of a house enjoyed a peaceful and prosperous life while some of his children later experienced misery and afflictions in the same place.

Even a good and strong horoscope cannot completely override the vaastu defects in a person's premises. The vaastu science based on the balance among the five elements of nature can help in bringing comfort, peace, harmony and prosperity to an extent which is permissible to its occupants by destiny.

Common Factors: There are three factors common to vaastu as well as astrology:

Planets

Directions

Elements

Before we analyse these three factors, let us underline the import of astrology. The vaastu experts need to master the science of astrology in order to relate the birth chart of the native with the premises he or she occupies. This will help in proper analysis of vaastu related problems and in suggesting effective remedies.

The same premises may be unlucky for an occupant but lucky for another and the reason lies in the different horoscopes they represent even though the map of the premises is the same.

It leads us to the three factors listed above:

(1) Planets: In vedic astrology we consider nine planets: Sun, Moon, Mars, Mercury, Jupiter, Venus, Saturn, Rahu and Ketu. Sun is not a planet but a star. In astrology and vaastu, however, it counts as a planet. Also Rahu and Ketu are not physically existing planets but two nodal points where the path of moon intercepts the path of earth.

In vaastu, all planets except ketu represent particular directions as given in Table A- 4.1

(2) Directions: In vaastu, eight directions are used to represent sides or corners of a plot of land and these are: north, east, south and west and then four directions as per the intersection of main directions ,viz. northeast, southeast, southwest and northwest.

In astrology also the birth chart is generally shown representing the four main directions, viz. north, east, west and south but in order to relate the birth chart to a plot of land or premises we can consider the remaining four directions, viz. northeast, southeast, southwest and northwest. These four later represent two houses each in a birth chart as indicated in the following table:

Table A 4.1: Relation among Vaastu-Directions, Planets and the Houses of a Birth Chart

Direction	Abbreviation	Hindi name as used in Vaastu	Governing planet in Vaastu	House represented in the birth chart
East	E	Poorv	Sun	1st (Ascendant or *Lagna*)
Northeast	NE	Eshaan	Jupiter	2nd and 3rd
North	N	Uttar	Mercury	4th
Northwest	NW	Vayavya	Moon	5th and 6th
West	W	Paschim	Saturn	7th
Southwest	SW	Nairtya	Rahu	8th and 9th
South	S	Dakshin	Mars	10th
Southeast	SE	Aagneya	Venus	11th and 12th

(3) Elements: Vaastu recognises five elements, viz. air, water, earth, fire and *aakaash*. The last one is a non-physical and finer element. It is believed that all space is filled with this element called Aakaash.

These elements are assigned specific areas in a plot of land as shown in the diagram of Figure A-4.1

In astrology we consider only four elements, viz. air, water, earth and fire. The Table A-4.2 gives the astrological classification of planets, signs and the houses of a chart relating to these four elements.

Table A 4.2: Astrological classification of Planets, Signs and Houses relating with the Four Elements

Element Represented	Planets	Zodiacal Signs	Houses of a Kaalpurush Kundali
Air	Saturn, Rahu	Gemini, Libra, Aquarius	3rd, 7th, 11th
Water	Moon, Venus	Cancer, Scorpio, Pisces	4th, 8th, 12th
Earth	Mercury	Taurus, Virgo, Capricorn	2nd, 6th, 10th
Fire	Sun, Mars	Aries, Leo, Sagittarius	1st, 5th, 9th

Note: Kaalpurush Kundali is an Aries ascendant chart. Here the signs tally with the numbers of houses they fall into, for example the 3rd, 7th, and 11th zodiacal signs, viz. Gemini, Libra and Aquarius fall respectively in 3rd, 7th and 11th houses.

However the same houses carry the elemental essence in charts of all other ascendant signs. To explain this point we can say that in a chart of any ascendant sign the houses

2nd, 6th and 10th are of earthy nature irrespective of the signs falling in these, and so for other houses.

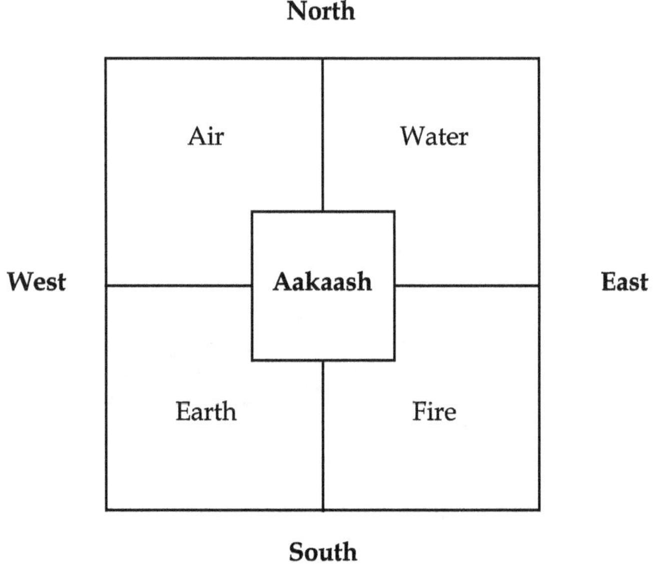

**Fig. A 4.1: Areas assigned to the five elements in
a plot of land.**

A vaastu consultant normally studies the birth chart of the occupant of premises. In case some particular house in the birth chart is under any negative influence, a vaastu dosha (defect) is not improbable in the corresponding direction as per Table A-4.1 The same is also true conversely the other way round, if a premises has some vaastu defect in a specific direction, there are chances of affliction in relevant house of the birth chart of that native.

5

How to Detect the Vaastu Defect?

The movement of planets and constellations influences our lives, so do the characteristics of our place of residence and work.

The positive vibrations of a place usher peace and progress in the lives of its occupants, while the negative vibrations tend to create obstacles and difficulties.

For knowing whether or not a vaastu dosha (defect) exists certainly in your premises, the person concerned should closely observe their day-to-day life. Solution is possible only after the problem is diagnosed.

If despite all efforts one is denied the desired results in life. If you get opportunities but nothing solid and beneficial materialises and one is deprived of all mental peace and contentment, then it could be owing to a vaastu defect either at their place of work or residence.

A vaastu defect at a work place affects all people working there and hinders the overall progress. There are many examples of prospering organisations coming to dramatic and sudden bankruptcy, loss or closure.

A vaastu defect at a living place, irrespective of the outward show and decency of that place, ruins the lives of its occupants. The residents face difficulties, litigation and health problems.

Sometimes a person disposes his old house where he was living happily and shifts to a new house and lands in troubles.

In any shopping complex there may be so many shops. While some shops run quite well, doing a good business, others fail to attract customers and run into losses. There may seem no logical explanation for this, but such things do happen around us.

A shop having positive vibrations and energy attracts customers and earns profit while a shop with negative energy faces problems and losses.

An architect can design and ensure a beautiful, well ventilated and good building but cannot guarantee peace and prosperity to its occupants. But at the time of purchasing a plot and planning construction, an expert guidance from a vaastu consultant can ensure progress and peace for its occupants provided important things like *mahurata* are also taken care of.

A competent vaastu consultant takes into consideration the type of soil, plot shape, adjoining areas, adjoining roads, magnetic fields, cosmic energy, sun rays, gravitational energy, etc., before recommending it to his or her client. If there are any defects, the consultant suggests certain remedies to ward off any negative effects.

Thus a close observation of life will enable a person to assess the situation and act accordingly.

6

Relevance and Benefits of Vaastu

Being an ancient science is vaastu relevant in today's ultra-modern and fast mode of life? This question occurs to the minds of many inquisitive people. Expert vaastu consultants and thousands of their satisfied clients certify that vaastu is very much relevant and applicable in the present milieu.

Falsity does not last long enough, only truth prevails. The ever increasing popularity of this great science testifies its feasibility.

Here are some spheres and aspects of life which benefit from vaastu:

Health: The greatest gift to a person is good health. Only a healthy and strong person succeeds in different walks of life and enjoys it to the fullest. Besides the personal hygienic habits the vaastu compatibility of premises ensures sound physical and mental health to its occupants.

In this regard, the main focus should be on keeping

the central part of the house as clean and tidy as possible. This central part known in vaastu as the *Brahmasthana* (place of Brahma) represents the stomach of the vaastu purush and the significance of stomach in keeping good health is no secret.

Relationships: Man is a social being and depends upon multiple relations with others. The health of our relationships goes a long way in determining the success and contentment in our lives.

In joint families many members live under a common roof and good relations among them is vital. Vaastu plays an important role in infusing and maintaining warmth in these relationships. Taking care of the north, east and north-east directions and keeping them defect free ensures to a greater extent the harmony among various members of a family.

Timely marriage: Timely marriage of daughters is highly imperative. And vaastu plays a crucial role in this regard. Yes, it does. An expert vaastu consultant will advise the client to take advantage of the north-west direction in this matter. This direction being under the planet moon is unstable in nature. If a marriageable daughter is residing in this part her timely marriage is predicted.

Peace of mind: Peace is eluding people these days because of their hectic lifestyle. Enjoying a life of bliss and progress depends largely on peace of mind. We cannot dictate peace in the external world, but if we invite and entertain peace within, at least we can expect a betterment of our outlook on life and surroundings. Also the peace within radiates all around.

Vaastu plays an important role in bringing and maintaining peace of mind. Living in vaastu dosha (defect) free premises is a boon.

According to the science of vaastu the north, north-east and east directions are a gateway to positive and rejuvenating energy. These directions should be taken care of to achieve peace and tranquillity.

The auspicious placement of the main entrance of a house can ensure a restful and peaceful night to its residents after a hectic day.

Overall Success: The main entrance of a house plays an important role. For all worldly activities one has to go out through the main door of his or her house. Therefore the auspiciousness of the main door cannot be ignored.

By fulfilling the vaastu requirements one can enjoy peace, health and prosperity and save undue expenses on medical bills and debts.

7

Frequently asked Questions about Vaastu

Various questions related to vaastu shastra have been answered in detail throughout this book. This chapter has been included to give short answers to some frequently asked questions.

Q1: What is Vaastu Shastra?

Answer: It is an ancient Hindu art and science of constructing buildings in harmony with forces of nature in order to bring and maintain peace of mind, health and prosperity to the occupants.

Q2: Does Vaastu Guarantee Prosperity?

Answer: Vaastu guides us to live in tune with the laws of nature and thus removes all obstacles coming in the way of our luck. But the destiny of a person, indicated by his or her birth chart decides the time and extent to which that individual can experience prosperity.

Q3: Is Vaastu Shastra meant for Hindus only?

Answer: Vaastu Shastra is a universal science independent of religion, caste and creed. It was developed by Hindus but it is for all.

Q4: What is the significance of Vaastu Purusha?

Answer: Vaastu Purusha is the soul or spirit of the premises. By following vaastu principles, one can prevent injury to Vaastu Purusha and ensure him respect and dignity.

Q5: What is the ideal shape of a plot?

Answer: A square having all four sides equal or a rectangular with length not more than twice its breadth are two ideal shapes for a plot for construction.

Q6: What is the basic difference between Vaastu and Feng Shui?

Answer: Vaastu guidelines are to be followed before planning and constructing a house whereas Feng Shui comes into play afterwards.

Q7: Why are corners important in Vaastu Shastra?

Answer: The corners represent meeting place for different directions and also elements. Because of these important factors corners are of great importance and must be without any defect.

Vaastu

8

Vaastu Purush and Mandalas

We support the belief that Lord Brahma is the original source of vaastu related knowledge that he taught. Lord Brahma gave that knowledge to Garg muni from whom it was passed on to Rishi Prashara and then to Brihidrath and finally to Vishwakarma.

The sage Vishwkarma through his treatise *Vishwakarma Prakaash* spread this knowledge for the benefit of all humanity.

The legend of vaastu purush as suggested by Vishwakarma

In *treta-yug* there appeared a huge demon who covered the whole sky. Any one who witnessed that frightful scene was shaken with fear. Even the devtaas were frightened and felt concerned. Led by Lord Indra, they approached Lord Brahma and expressed their concern and fears about that giant.

Lord Brahma blessed the devtaas with fearlessness and asked them to use their powers to throw the giant face down on the ground.

Thus assured and encouraged by Lord Brahma the devtaas with their divine powers brought the demon face down on the ground and kept him there. With such act of the devtaas Lord Brahma was pleased and granted the devtaas vaas or residence in the respective parts of the demon held by each.

Then the demon also approached Lord Brahma and complained that the devtaas had tortured him for none of his fault. Lord Brahma out of compassion blessed the demon and told him that he will be called vaastu purush and will rule plots of land. The lord assured him that before construction on a plot the owner will have to worship him or face obstacles and problems. The demon was equally pleased.

North

Fig. B 8.1: Vaastu Purush lying face-down on a plot of land.

What is vaastu purush in rational terms?

There are many variations to the legend of Vaastu Purush. Some believe that the demon was created out of the sweat of Lord Shiva. The demon then grew up gradually to immense dimensions.

There is no point in bickering over which legend is correct and which is not. We just need to understand the logic behind the concept of vaastu purush. In logical terms the vaastu purush is the 'spirit' or 'essence' which represents the omnipresent 'Prana' energy.

Our wise sages employed mythology or mythical tales to describe and explain the mysteries of the universe. We humans understand better things which relate to the human form. Understandably the deities we worship are depicted in human form.

Mythical stories are created to give concrete form to the formless and abstract. This is for the benefit of the common man to understand the complex forces at play.

The mythical story and concept of vaastu purush represents real hidden forces in a fictional form. The symbolism of vaastu purush represents the forces that are operational within a confined space.

Vaastu purush is the constituting simile for harmonising and synthesising the different forces at play on the cosmological, spiritual and architectural planes within a confined space.

The rationale behind the philosophy that the vaastu purush exists in every plot of land and structure is just a reminder that every plot of land or premises is a living organism vibrant with life, rhythm and harmony. A wonderful concept indeed propounded by our wise ancients! Our head naturally bows in respect to our sages and their wisdom!

The vaastu purush mandalas

As described and depicted above the vaastu purush is represented lying face down with his head in the north-east corner and feet in the south-west corner of a plot of land (refer Figure B-8.1).

The plot of land is divided into a number of square cells also known as grids. The sketch showing the vaastu purush lying face down on a plot of land divided into a number of square cells is called vaastu purush mandala or vaastu purush chakra.

In this context the 'purush' in general represents cosmic and environmental power, energy and causal force whereas the 'mandala' denotes the relationship between the purush and the plot of land.

Depending upon the application the plot of land is divided into certain number of square cells as described in the following Table:

Table B 8.1: Various *Vaastu Purush Mandalas* and their Applications

Mandala	Application
1 cell mandala called *Sakala*	For fire altars or *Havan- kundas*
64 cell mandala called *Manduka*	For temples
81 cell mandala called *Paramasyika*	For residential buildings
1024 cell mandala called *Indrakanta*	For planning a city

The 81-Cell Vaastu Mandala or Chakra

Let us elaborate here the 81 cell vaastu Mandala or chakra as used for residential plots.

For the names of the devtaas governing each part we refer to the chapter titled – 'Vastuvidyadhyaya' of the *Brihat*

Samhita by Acharya Varah Mihir. The Shlokas number 43 to 50 of this chapter as given below describe the names of the 45 different devtaas which govern various parts of this chakra:

'Shikhiparjanye jaiantendra suryesatya bhrishoantrikshashchai,
Aishanyadrikmasho dakshinpoorveyanilai kone.'

Shloka 43

'Poosha vitath brihtkshatyamgandharvakhye bhringrajmriga,
pitridowariksugreevkusumdantambuptaisura.'

Shloka 44

'Shoshoath paapyakshama rogey kone tatoahimukhayo cha,
bhalaatsombhujgastoaditir diti riti kramshai.'

Shloka 45

'Madhye brahma navkoshthkadhipoasyarma sthitey prachyam,
aikantraatpradkhshinmasmaat savita vivisshavasaye.'

Shloka 46

'Vivudhadhipatitasmaanmitroanyo rajakshamnama cha,
prithvidharapavatsavityeye brahmna paridho.'

Shloka 47

'Aapo nameshaney kone hotashaney cha savitrai,
jai iti cha nairitaye rudr anileyabhantarpadaishu.'

Shloka 48

'Aapastthaivatsey parjanyoarganraditishachai vargoayam,
aivam kone kone padika shayu panch panch sura.'

Shloka 49

'Bahiya dwipda sheshastey vibudha vinshati samakhyata,
sheshashachatvaroanye tripda dwiksharmadyastey.'

Shloka 50

The above shlokas infer as follows:

'Starting with the north-east corner in the outer cells these *devtas* are Shikhi, Parjanya, Jayant, Indra, Surya, Satya, Bhrish, Antriksha and Anil. These 9 *devtas* are situated in 9 cells from the north-east corner to the south-east corner.

Then from south-east corner to the south-west corner the *devtas* are Poosha, Vitath, Britkshat, Yam, Gandharv, Bhringraj, Mrig and Pitri.

Then along the western side these are Dovarik, Sugreev, Pushpdant, Varun, Asur, Shosh, Paapyakshama and Roga.

In the northern side the *devtas* are Naag, Mukhya, Bhalaat, Soma, Bhujag, Aaditi and Diti.

The central 9 cells belong to Brahma. Above this in the east there is *Ayarma* in three cells and in the three cells on south side is *Vivasvan*. The three western cells belong to *Mitr* and the three northern cells to *Prithvidhar*.

The remaining cells in the north-east belong to *Aapvats*, in south-east to *Savita*, in southwest to *Indra* and in north-west to Rajyakshama.

Apart from these *devtas* all those belonging to the outermost rows also govern the adjacent cell in the 2nd inner row.

In other words Jayant, Indra, Surya, Satya and Bhrish in the east Vitath, Brikshat, Yam, Gandharv, Bhringraj in the south Sugreev, Kusumdant, Varun, Asur, Shosh in the west and Mukhya, Bhalaat, Soma, Bhujag and Aditi in the north have lordship of two cells each. Apart from these Ayarma, Vivasvan, Mitr, Prithvidhar have lordship of three cells each. The sketch below shows an 81 cell mandala with names of deities.

North

Shikhi 1	Diti 32	Aaditi 31	Bhujag 30	Soma 29	Bhalaat 28	Mukhya 27	Nag 26	Roga 25
Parjanya 2	Aap 33	Aaditi 31	Bhujag 30	Soma 29	Bhalaat 28	Mukhya 27	Rudra 36	Paapyakshama 24
Jayant 3	Jayant 3	Aapvats 44	Prithvidhar 43	Prithvidhar 43	Prithvidhar 43	Rajyakshama 42	Shosh 23	Shosh 23
Indra 4	Indra 4	Ayarma 37	Brahma 45	Brahma 45	Brahma 45	Mitrr 41	Asur 22	Asur 22
Surya 5	Surya 5	Ayarma 37	Brahma 45	Brahma 45	Brahma 45	Mitrr 41	Varun 21	Varun 21
Satya 6	Satya 6	Ayarma 37	Brahma 45	Brahma 45	Brahma 45	Mitrr 41	Pushpdant 20	Pushpdant 20
Bhrish 7	Bhrish 7	Savita 38	Vivasvaan 39	Vivasvaan 39	Vivasvaan 39	Indra 40	Sugreev 19	Sugreev 19
Antriksh 8	Saavitr	Vitath 11	Brihtkhshat 12	Yam 13	Gandharv 14	Bhringraj 15	Jai 35	Dovaarik 18
Anil 9	Poosha 10	Vitath 11	Brihitkshat 12	Yam 13	Gandharv 14	Bhringraj 15	Mrig 16	Pitrr 17

South

Fig. B 8.2: Places Assigned to *Devtas* (Deities) in an 81 square *Vaastu Purush Mandala*.

This mandala or chakra is used to determine the character of a particular area in a plot of land depending upon the nature of the devta governing that part.

Notably some devtas govern areas covering more than one cell. The central nine cells are governed by Lord Brahma.

9

Vaastu and Elements

The five elements, viz. earth, water, air, fire and aakaash are connected to life like breath. The whole physical cosmos is created out of these elements.

If appropriate measures are adopted to keep these elements in balance at the time of construction, then the subtle and electromagnetic energies so produced would contribute to one's health and harmony. This is so because our bodies are also composed of the same five elements.

Although the five elements permeate our physical body, yet these are assigned certain distinct places. The water element is seated in the feet, earth in the knees, air in the umbilical, fire in the shoulders and aakaash in the cerebrum.

Whenever these elements in our body are out of balance or their flow is obstructed for any reason, disharmony, tension and lack of peace ensue. The same applies to a plot of land.

The illustration shows the areas in a plot of land governed by different elements.

These elements are described below along with their import in respect of vaastu:

Earth: This element is integral to life. The earth acts like a huge magnet with its north and south poles. The gravitational force of the earth impacts all life.

Before the actual construction is undertaken the worship of the earth (*Bhoomi Poojan*) should be performed as a rule. Proper selection of plot helps in keeping the earth element in balance.

Water: Water is essential for existence of all life on earth. Three fourth of the earth is surrounded by water. Water consists of oxygen and hydrogen. By proper management of water storage and drainage in premises this element can be kept balanced for harmony.

Fire: Fire is a fuel that helps in cooking food to satisfy hunger. Fire also gives light and heat. The sun is the major and original source of fire. In our culture this element is central to all auspicious ceremonies.

The fire element (*Agni*) resides in the south-east corner of a plot. By locating all fire and electrical equipment in this direction fire element can be kept in balance.

Air: Air is a valuable gift of nature. All life on this planet needs air to survive. A vast band of atmosphere surrounds the earth and contains many gases such as nitrogen, oxygen, carbon dioxide and carbon monoxide and dust and water vapours, etc. Life on earth is regulated by the properties of all these constituents.

Proper air circulation in a building is ensured by planning doors, windows and ventilators at appropriate places and directions and is essential to prevent any vaastu defect.

Aakaash: This fine element fills virtually all empty spaces. Some uncovered space in the north and north-east directions is advisable to allow enough of this fine element into the premises.

As the central portion called the brahmasthan is the abode of this element, in Rajasthan it is customary to keep this portion empty.

10

Vaastu and Natural Forces

We are surrounded by many visible as well as invisible forces, which directly or indirectly affect life and vaastu recognises them in due measure. These forces or energies are described below:

1. Celestial Energy
2. Gravitational Energy
3. Magnetic Energy
4. Solar Energy
5. Ultraviolet Energy
6. Infrared Energy
7. Subtle Energies

1. Celestial energy: Celestial Energy is broad spectrum energy received on earth from the cosmos or outer space, and is generally called cosmic energy.

A great part of this energy originates in stars due to certain changes in them. Some energy comes constantly while some comes out in occasional powerful bursts.

Lethal doses of cosmic energy are luckily stopped from reaching us by the presence of atmosphere around our planet.

The earth's axis is tilted at an angle of $23.5°$ from the vertical. Due to earth's tilt, its rotation on this axis and its revolution around the sun, harmful cosmic energies arrive in greater intensity from the south and south-west directions.

This is one of the main reasons why these two directions are considered inauspicious in vaastu. However, this book suggests best utilisation of these directions in order to fill the premises with positive energy.

2. Gravitational energy: An object thrown upward with force would fall down with the diminishing of the upward force.

Normally we do not pay any attention to this simple fact of things falling down, but it caused the great scientist Newton to scratch his head and discover the reason.

Once Newton was sitting under an apple tree and an apple fell down. He was at that time in a contemplative mood so even this every day occurrence caused him to think deeper. He reasoned why the apple fell down and not went upward into the sky. Aware that nature's secrets are revealed only through inquiry, he contemplated and concluded that probably earth exerts some kind of pull on all objects. Later he mathematically derived equations and this pulling energy was given the name of gravitation.

Not only our earth but all objects exert this gravitational pull on other objects, greater the mass of an object greater is its gravitational pull. All planets and stars have their gravitational force. Moon being quite close to earth, exerts noticeable gravitational effect on it and its inhabitants.

3. Magnetic energy: We all have seen and experimented with a magnet in our school laboratory. A magnet attracts all magnetic materials such as iron.

A magnet has two poles: the north pole, and the south pole. If we have two magnets then their like poles (north-north or south-south) repel each other while the unlike poles (north-south) attract each other.

Some simple experiments reveal that invisible lines of force between the two poles of a magnet exist in a specific pattern around it. This region around a magnet within which its force acts is called its magnetic field. The stronger the magnet the farther its field extends.

Our earth acts like a huge natural magnet with its magnetic north and south poles located near its geographic poles. An instrument called magnetic compass is used to determine these poles and other directions. The red marked end of the needle of a magnetic compass points towards the geographic north pole of the earth.

As magnetic lines of force of the earth magnet pass through all premises, the science of vaastu tackles this phenomenon by defining the characteristics of directions of a plot of land. The magnetic field affects us because our bodies have traces of many metals such as iron, zinc, and copper, etc.

In addition to the earth's magnetic field the magnetic field of the sun also influences life on earth.

4. Solar energy: The energy spectrum is quite broad but only a narrow band of energies is visible to us. This visible part of the spectrum consists of light of different colours from red at one end to violet at the other. The natural light of the sun contains all these hues. A glass prism causes the natural light to split into its various coloured constituents. Under suitable conditions the water drops suspended in the atmosphere on a rainy day act as tiny prisms and split the light of the sun producing a rainbow in the sky.

Our great wise sages realised the positive effects of the mild rays of the rising sun on the life on earth and therefore attached importance to the north-east and east directions in particular.

Heat and light from the sun are essential for sustenance of all life on earth.

5. Ultraviolet energy: The early morning rays of the sun contain ultraviolet energy which is low in heat content but rich in Vitamin D. The UV energy destroys bacteria and purifies the environment. The maximum entry of UV energy in premises can be ensured by keeping the walls on east light and low in height. It is better to avoid any trees and buildings in the east of a house.

6. Infrared energy: As the sun moves towards the west during the day the sun rays become rich in the infrared energy. The Infrared rays are harmful because of high heat content. By keeping the western and southern walls thick and high one can avoid entry of these rays. It is good if there are high hills in these directions.

7. Subtle energies: Besides the coarse forms of energy described above there are subtle or finer energies no less significant.

Researchers have detected very mild magnetic fields around human bodies and brain in particular. It seems the two hemispheres of our brain act as two poles of a natural magnet.

The magnetic and electric fields are interrelated. An ECG machine helps doctors track the electrical activity of the heart. Similarly, an ECG machine can show various waveforms connected with magnetic and electric activity of the brain.

Fig. B 10.1: Subtle lines of magnetic energy around our head

The planets and stars also affect life on earth and the great science of astrology is all about these effects. Vaastu being related to astrology also takes into account these celestial influences by assigning planets the lordship of various directions of a plot of land as described in the Table A 4.1 of chapter four of section-A of this book.

Conclusively, vaastu is not just a speculative thought; rather it is based on scientific facts.

11

Vaastu and Directions

This book primarily aims to convey that the right use of vaastu can harmonise our lives.

This chapter describes the common defects or as they are called vaastu doshas for each of the eight directions of a premises. General remedies for alleviating those defects are also prescribed.

The eight directions discussed here are: (1) North, (2) East, (3) South, (4) West, (5) North-east, (6) South-east, (7) South-west, (8) North-west

The North Direction

In the domain of vaastu, the north direction is considered very auspicious. This direction is attributed to the water and air elements. Flowing water in this direction gives prosperity.

According to the principles of vaastu a house should face north or a shop facing north will attract wealth.

In general this direction brings prosperity, progress, relaxation and peace of mind; it also promises sexual bliss and strong marital bond, spiritual pursuits such as success in meditation and self-awareness.

Table below gives some salient features of this direction.

Table B 11.1: Salient features of North direction

Deity	Governing Planet	Elements	Favourable Colour
Kuber (Lord of wealth) and Soma (Lord of Health)	Mercury	Air and Water	Green

Guidelines for harmonising the north direction

1. A kitchen in this part may lead to quarrels in the house. If there is kitchen beside a bathroom in this direction then women of the house quarrel with each other.

2. Garbage and junk material in this part is best avoided. This will prevent any kind of monetary loss to the occupants of the premises.

3. Undue expenses and debts can be prevented by keeping this direction lower in level as compared to the central part. This simple precaution will bring harmony and peace.

4. There may be loss of property if there is no empty space left between the northern boundary wall and the covered area, particularly so if instead of the north the empty space exists in the south. There should be more empty space in the north than in the south.

5. Locating underground water storage in the north part helps in achieving spiritual powers. Locate swimming pool, fountains, underground water tank, well, etc., on the north side of the diagonal line between the north-east and south-west corners.

The East Direction

Being the direction of sunrise, it is considered very auspicious. Vaastu claims that this direction gives contentment, enthusiasm, optimistic feelings and inspiration.

Table B 11.2: Salient Features of East Direction

Deity	Governing Planet	Elements	Favourable Colour
Indra (King of gods)	The Sun	Fire and Water	Orange

Guidelines for harmonising the east direction

1. Some empty space in this direction promises healthy male progeny. There should be more empty space in east than in west.

2. In case the house is east-facing and there is a road in the east, then any open space in the western part should not be lower than the eastern level. Taking care of this important point will prevent lingering diseases to the male members.

3. A toilet in east is better avoided. Otherwise the occupants may suffer from health problems.

4. Financial losses can be prevented if the east direction is free from rubbish or waste materials lying in heaps. Keeping this direction clean also helps in the wellbeing of progeny.

5. Poverty can be prevented by keeping the slope towards east. This also saves from eye diseases and paralysis.

6. For safety of the progeny, the eastern boundary wall should be lower than that in the west.

7. The occupants of a house live longer and do not get depressed, if there is no blockage in this direction, allowing the flow of positive energy.

8. Plant basil (*Tulsi*) in east direction.

The South Direction

In the domain of vaastu, the south direction is not considered auspicious. In fact, the vaastu treatises indicate mixed results for this direction. But the modern progressive thought suggests ways of reducing the negative effects by certain methods and precautions.

Table B 11.3: Salient features of South direction

Deity	Governing Planet	Elements	Favourable Colour
Yama (Lord of Death)	Mars	Fire and Earth	Red

Guidelines for harmonising the south direction

1. As the negative vibrations are supposed to enter premises from this direction, the south boundary walls and walls of the building should be strong, thick and higher than those of the north.

2. The southern levels should be higher than those of the central part of the house to ensure good health to the occupants and to keep the expenses under control.

3. Empty spaces in this direction are better avoided to prevent financial problems and lack of harmony.

4. In case there exists a south-facing main entrance and it is not feasible to shift it, then it should be ensured that there is no open space or poorly lit area in front of the entrance. These measures will also benefit the brothers and sisters of the owner.

5. A place for worship (*pooja* room) in this direction is never advised.

The West Direction

The sun sets in the west at the end of a day. All those who work during the day look forward to a relaxing night. After a peaceful and relaxing night we all feel full of renewed energy and enthusiasm. So the view that this direction gives prosperity but it lacks in stability.

Table B 11.4: Salient features of West direction

Deity	Governing Planet	Elements	Favourable Colour
Varun (Lord of Air)	Saturn	Air and Earth	Blue

Guidelines for harmonising the west direction

1. It is a bad idea to locate a kitchen in this direction. Doing so causes difficulties in saving money.

2. Locating a bathroom or master bedroom in the west part causes undesired travelling and marital problems.

3. The slopes of the floor should not be towards this direction as it can cause loss of fame and money.

4. If the waste water drains out through west direction it will cause diseases to the male members.

5. It is good for the male progeny if more empty space is left in the east than in the west direction.

The North-east Direction

This direction is believed to give prosperity, progress in all spheres of life and peace of mind.

Vaastu places great importance in this corner where two auspicious directions, viz. north and east meet.

Table B 11.5: Salient features of North-east direction

Deity	Governing Planet	Elements	Favourable Colour
Lord Shankar	Jupiter	Water	Yellow

Guidelines for harmonising the north-east direction

1. There should not be any ditch in this direction as it is believed to bring bad luck.
2. Financial losses and danger to progeny can be prevented by keeping the floor slope towards this direction.
3. A toilet in this direction may cause quarrels and damage to one's character.
4. A long life without any enemies is possible if heaps of waste materials in this direction are avoided.
5. This corner should not be deformed if one desires to enjoy harmony and wealth and to be blessed with male progeny.

The South-east Direction

Vaastu relates the health of the house owner with south-east corner.

If this direction is free of defects, then the fire element is kept fairly balanced and occupants enjoy a peaceful, healthy, comfortable and contented life.

Table B 11.6: Salient features of Southeast direction

Deity	Governing Planet	Elements	Favourable Colour
Agni (Fire)	Venus	Fire	Dull White

Guidelines for harmonising the south-east direction

1. This direction suits well for a kitchen but is most unfavourable for building an underground water storage tank or a well. If such a tank or well exists along with a kitchen, then it may cause health problems to the housewife.
2. An entrance in this corner brings disharmony and danger of thieves.
3. Building a kitchen in this direction is a good idea provided that its walls and ceiling are in good condition and receive repair. Otherwise, the housewife may face various problems and ill health.

The South-west Direction

Vaastu norms require that this direction should be free of defects; otherwise one may land into troubles all of a sudden.

Table B 11.7: Salient features of South-west direction

Deity	Governing Planet	Elements	Favourable Colour
Nritti	Rahu	Earth	Blue

Guidelines for harmonising the south-west direction

1. There should not be any gap, crack, or broken part in the south-west wall, or else the occupants may be possessed by evil spirits.
2. This corner should not be empty or light in weight. If so, one finds it difficult to maintain a good bank balance.
3. Locating a well, underground water tank or a ditch in this part causes health problems.
4. Keeping the ground level of south-west higher than that of north-east incurs the danger of enemies.
5. If rain or waste water collected in this area is drained out through the south direction, females suffer and if that water is drained out through west direction, males suffer.
6. Any extensions to this corner may cause debts, litigation and danger of enemies.

The North-west Direction

Vaastu considers this as an auspicious direction. For enjoying prosperity, good health and long life it is imperative to keep this direction free from vaastu doshas.

Table B 11.8: Salient features of North-west direction

Deity	Governing Planet	Elements	Favourable Colour
Vaayu(Air)	The Moon	Air	White

Guidelines for harmonising the north-west direction

1. A bedroom in this corner may cause health problems and poverty.

2. A kitchen here creates mental instability in females.
3. A study room in this corner is responsible for lack of concentration and interest.
4. A garden or potted plants kept in this direction usher good luck and spiritual inclinations.
5. The slope of the ground should be from north-west to north-east for enjoying good health and freedom from litigation.
6. Those buying a already built house should ensure there are no defects in this direction, because the lord of this direction, viz. the moon occupies a place of great importance in one's life.
7. All pet animals or birds should be kept in the north-west corner.

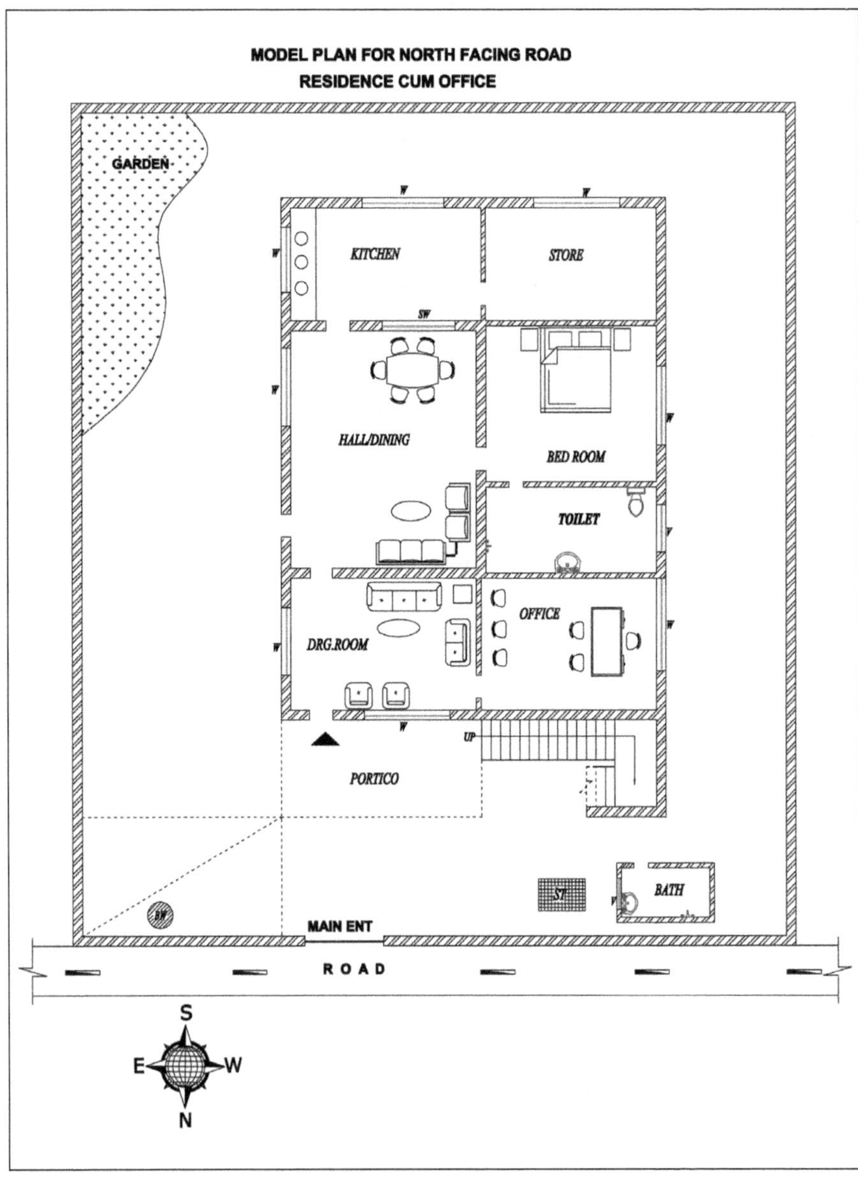
MODEL PLAN FOR NORTH FACING ROAD
RESIDENCE CUM OFFICE
GARDEN
KITCHEN
STORE
SW
HALL/DINING
BED ROOM
TOILET
DRG.ROOM
OFFICE
PORTICO
UP
BATH
ST
MAIN ENT
ROAD
S
E W
N

MODEL PLAN FOR NORTH FACING ROAD

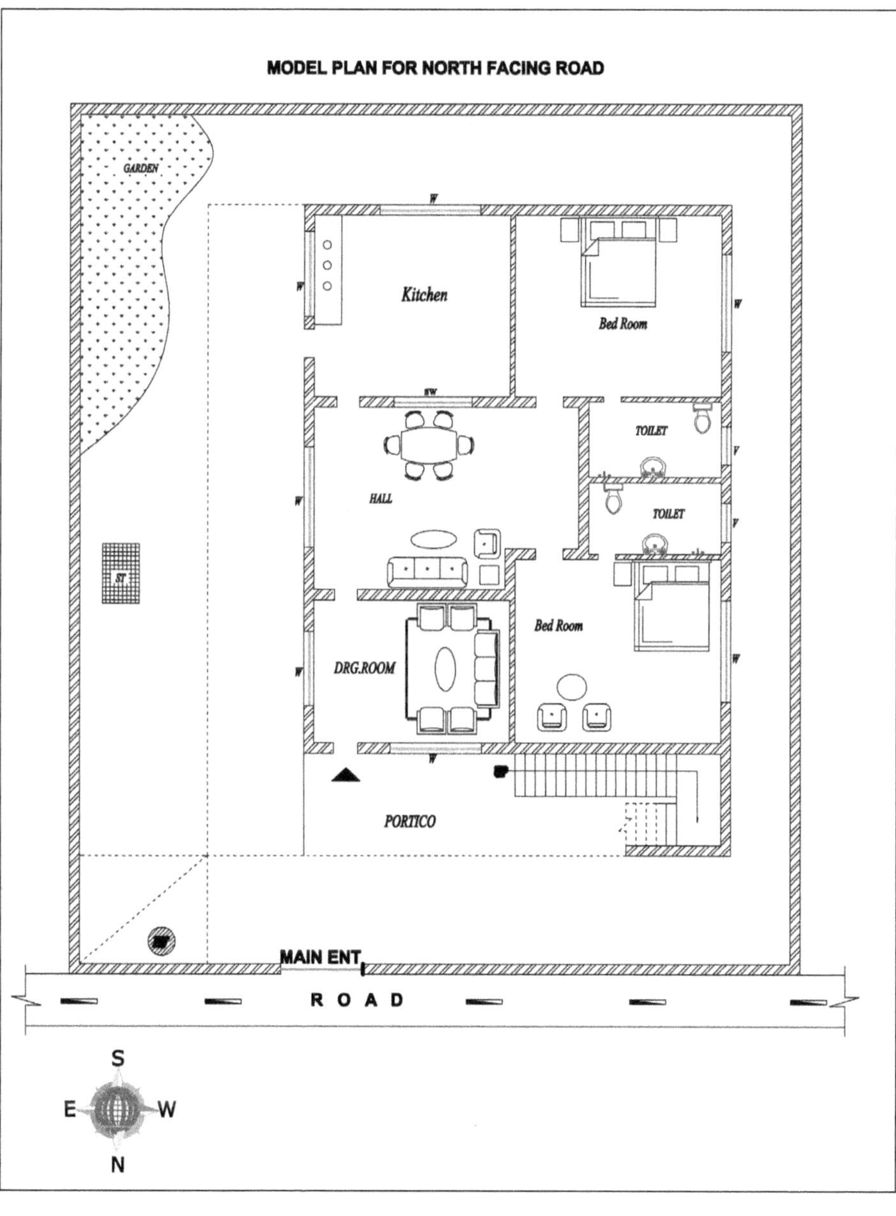

82

MODEL PLAN FOR SOUTH FACING ROAD
ST
BATH
W.C.
KITCHEN
HALL
BED ROOM
BED ROOM
RECEPTION
GARDEN
Up
MAIN ENT
MAIN ENT
ROAD
N
W
E
S

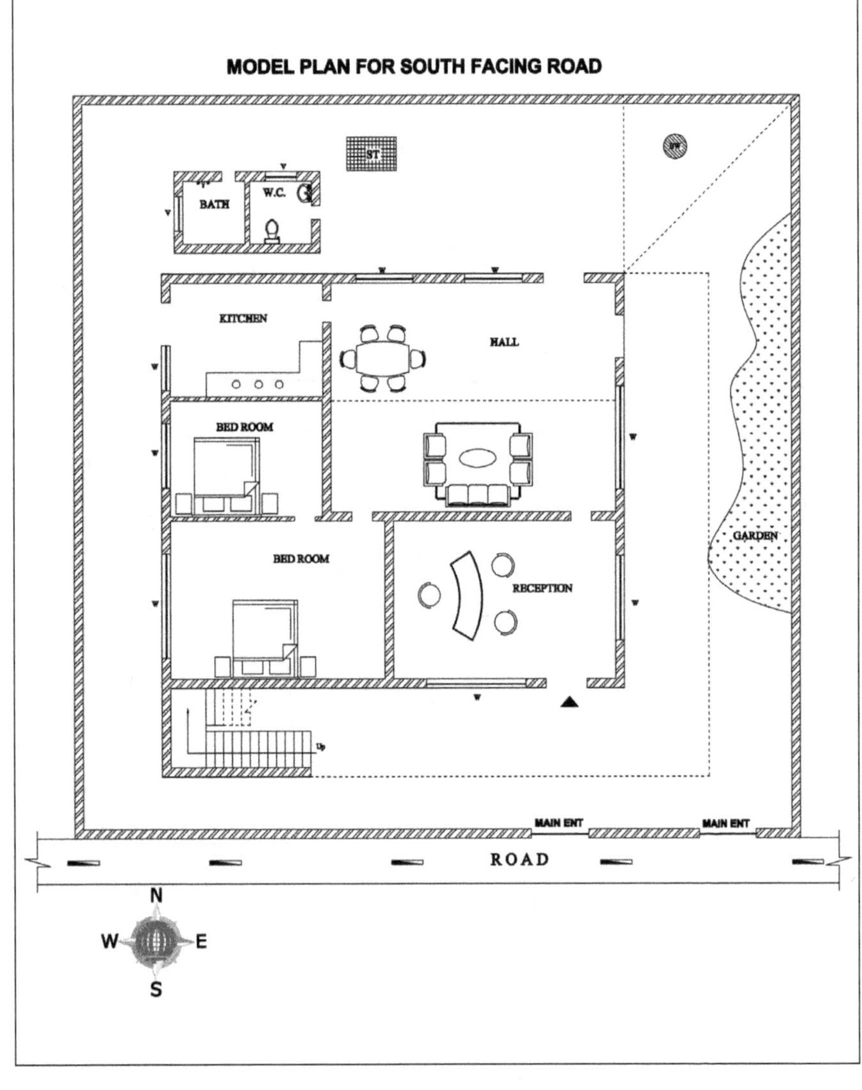

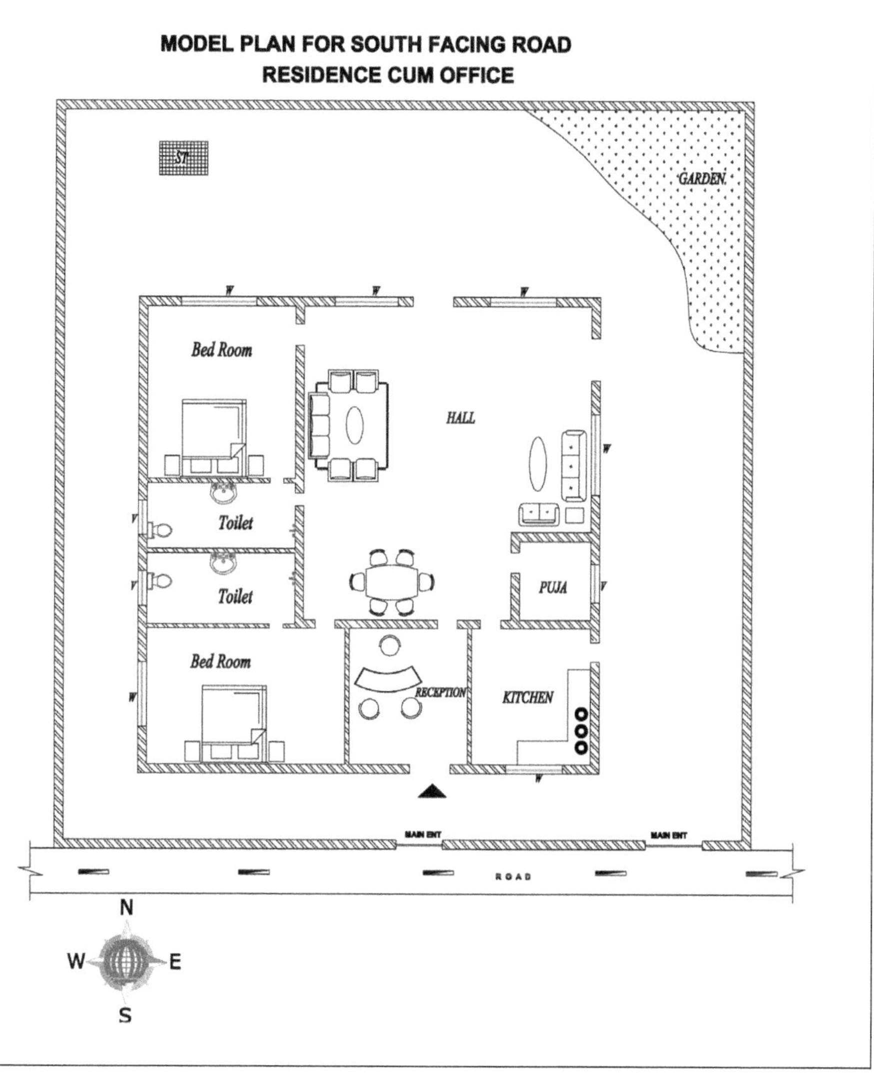

MODEL PLAN FOR SOUTH FACING ROAD
RESIDENCE CUM OFFICE
ST
GARDEN
Bed Room
HALL
Toilet
Toilet
PUJA
Bed Room
RECEPTION
KITCHEN
MAIN ENT
MAIN ENT
ROAD
N
W
E
S

MODEL PLAN FOR WEST FACING ROAD

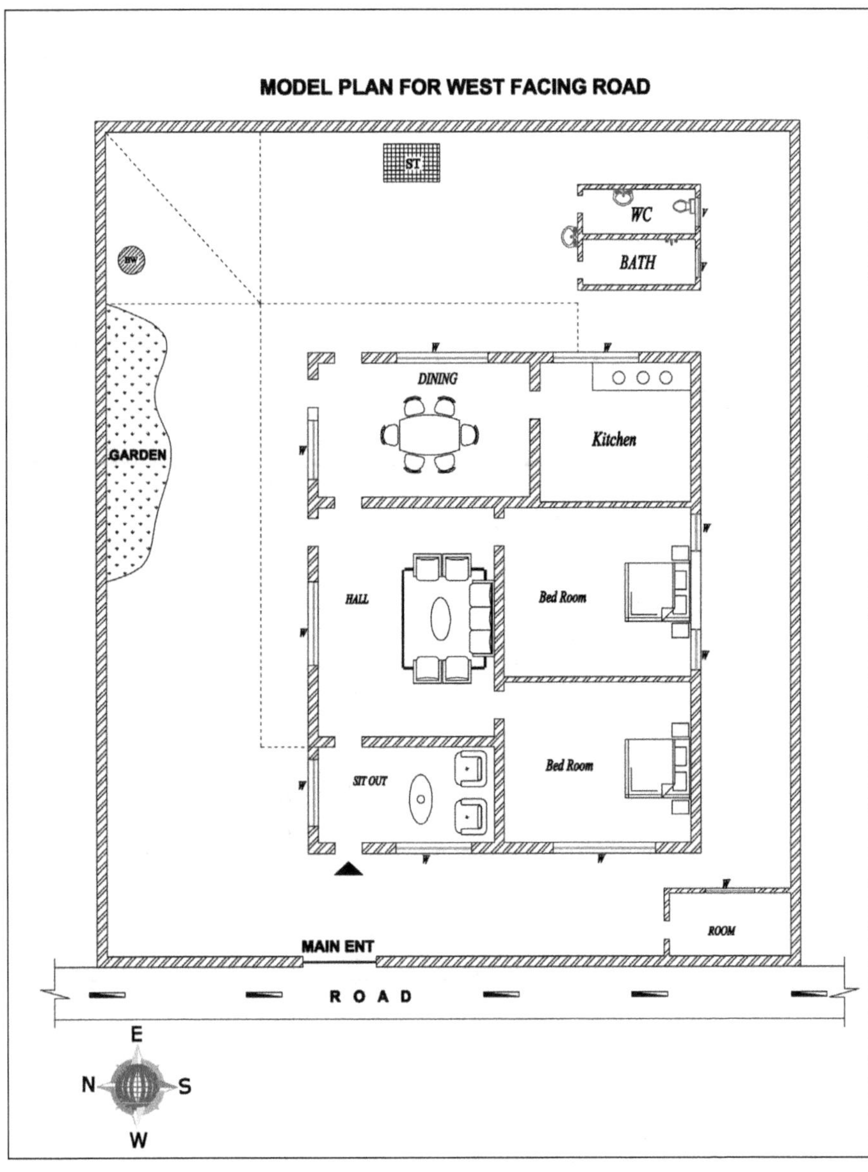

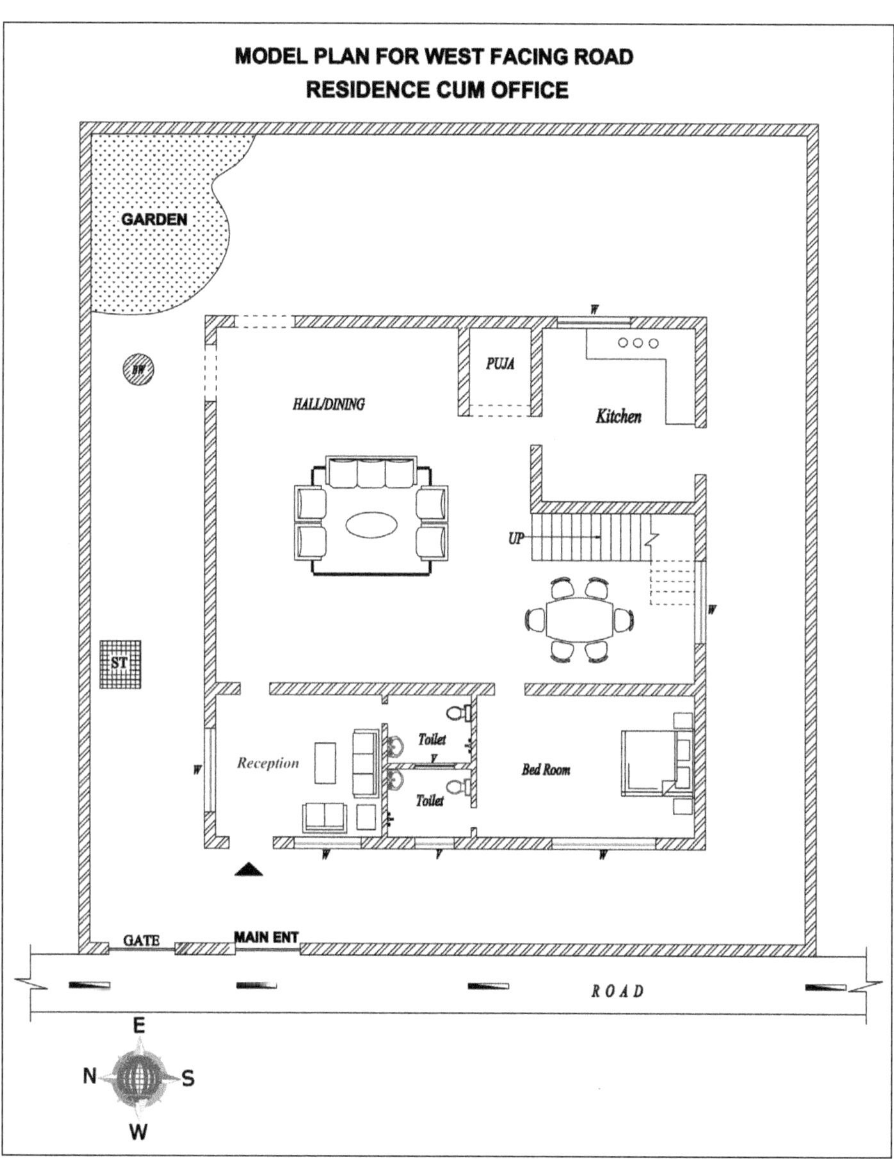

MODEL PLAN FOR WEST FACING ROAD
RESIDENCE CUM OFFICE
GARDEN
BW
PUJA
Kitchen
HALL/DINING
UP
ST
Reception
Toilet
Toilet
Bed Room
W
GATE
MAIN ENT
ROAD
E
N
S
W

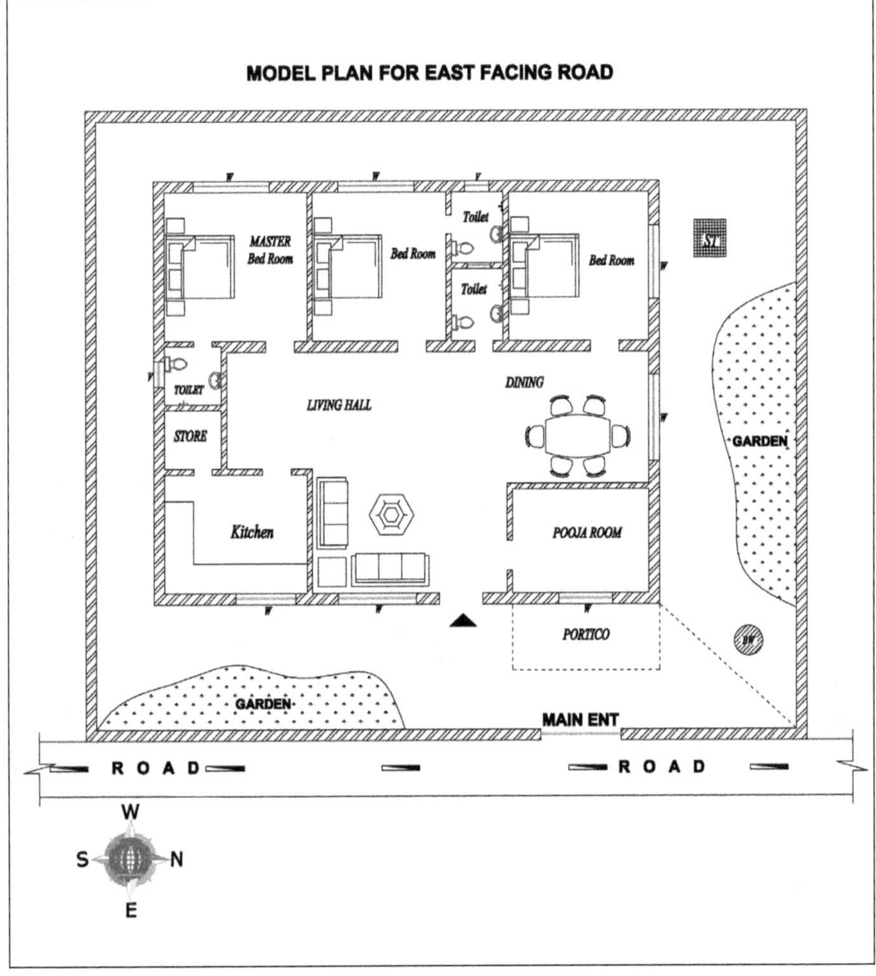

MODEL PLAN FOR EAST FACING ROAD
MASTER Bed Room
Bed Room
Toilet
Toilet
Bed Room
ST
TOILET
LIVING HALL
DINING
STORE
GARDEN
Kitchen
POOJA ROOM
GARDEN
PORTICO
BW
MAIN ENT
ROAD
ROAD
W
S
N
E

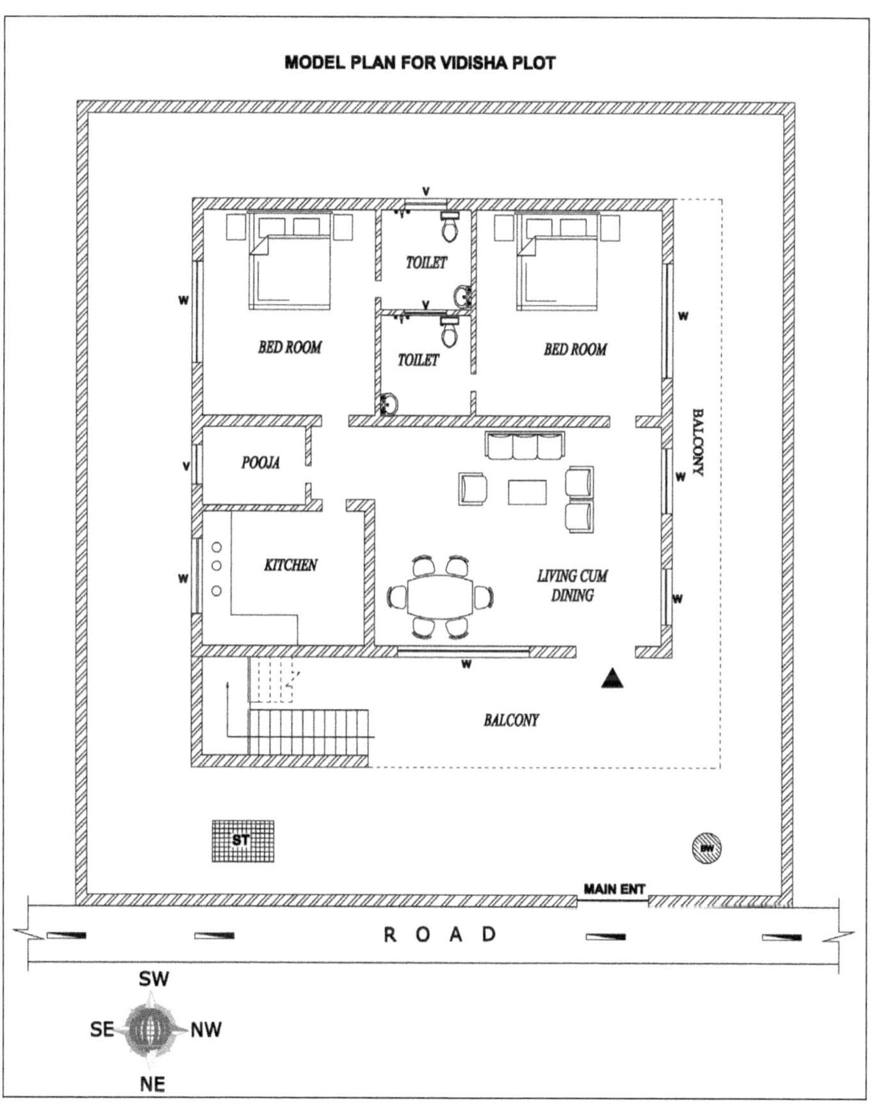

MODEL PLAN FOR VIDISHA PLOT
TOILET
BED ROOM
TOILET
BED ROOM
POOJA
BALCONY
KITCHEN
LIVING CUM DINING
BALCONY
ST
MAIN ENT
ROAD
SW
SE
NW
NE

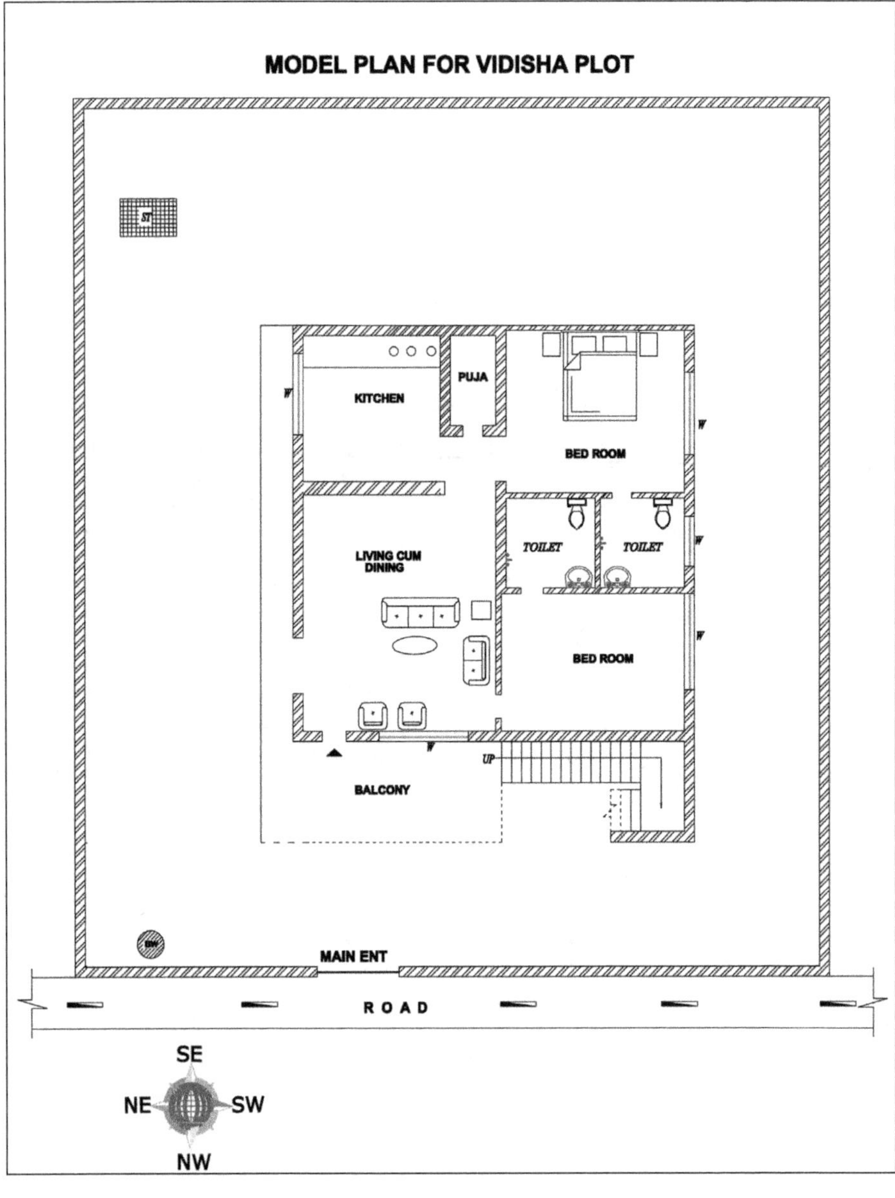

MODEL PLAN FOR VIDISHA PLOT
ST
PUJA
KITCHEN
W
BED ROOM
W
TOILET
TOILET
W
LIVING CUM DINING
W
BED ROOM
UP
W
BALCONY
MAIN ENT
ROAD
SE
NE
SW
NW

MODEL PLAN FOR VIDISHA PLOT

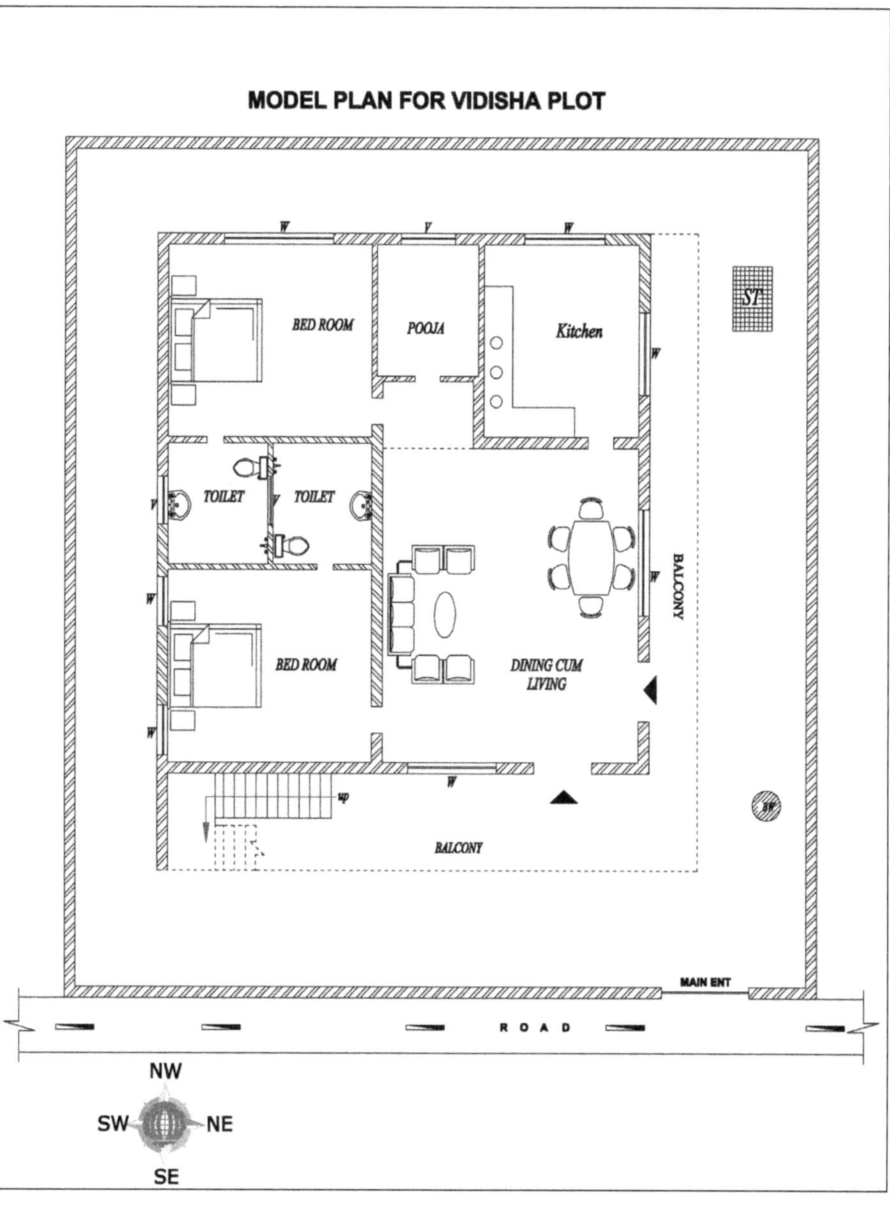

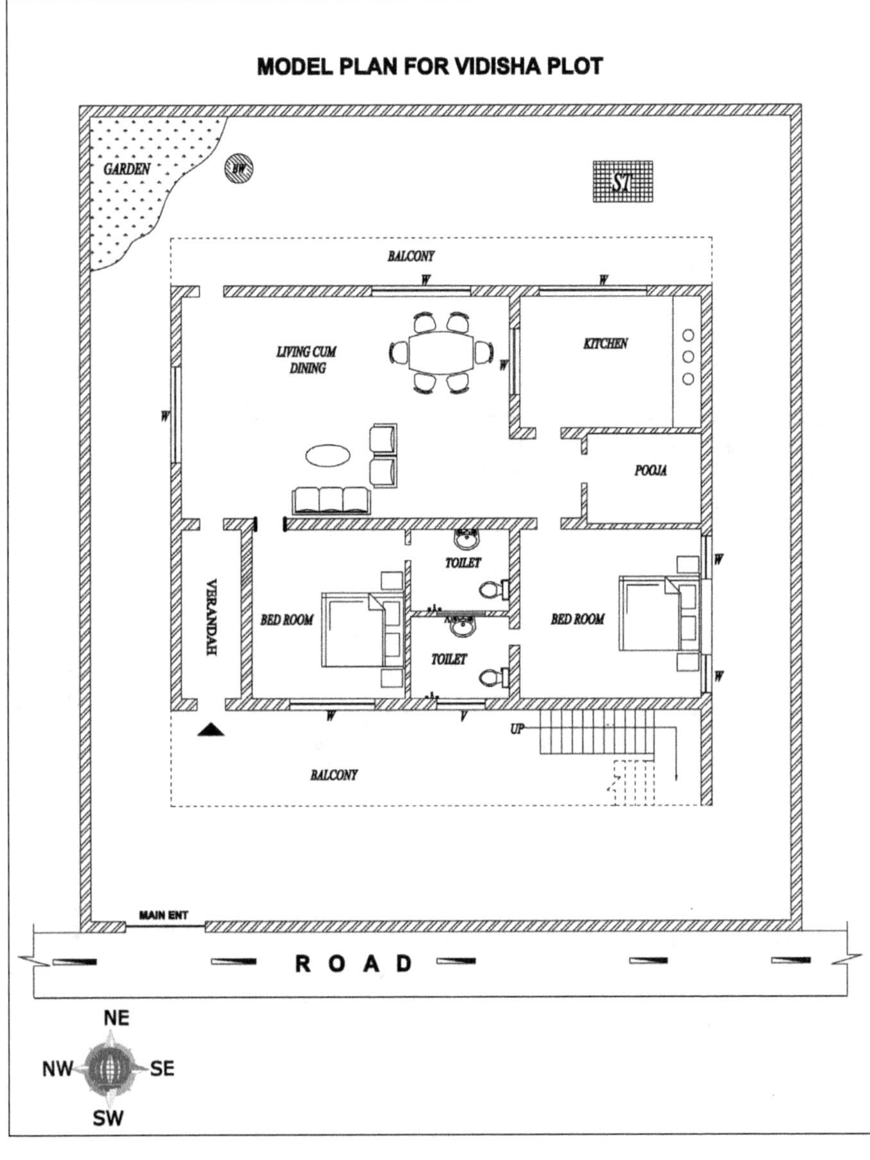

MODEL PLAN FOR VIDISHA PLOT
GARDEN
HW
ST
BALCONY
W
W
LIVING CUM DINING
KITCHEN
W
W
POOJA
W
W
TOILET
VERANDAH
BED ROOM
KW
BED ROOM
TOILET
W
W
W
V
UP
MAIN ENT
BALCONY
R O A D
NE
NW
SE
SW

12

Vaastu and Plots of Land

In the matter of selecting the right kind of plot of land for building a house, importance to judging the type of soil is also crucial.

According to the treatise *Brahamsamhita* the best plot of land for construction is that whose soil is fertile, well bound and solid and carries good aroma.

Four types of soil are described in our treatises:

Brahmani: A grassy land with good taste and aroma is called brahmani. This type of land is recommended for residential buildings and gives comfort to the occupants.

Khashamia: A reddish land with pungent taste is called khashamia. Such land is good for building police posts, courts and residence for government staff, etc.

Vaishya: This is a yellowish soil with sour taste. This is recommended for commercial activities related to cultivation, keeping animals, fisheries, storage of food products and dairies, etc. Also good for building banks, commercial complexes, showrooms, etc.

Shuda: This type of land is blackish with bitter taste and is not considered good for residential purposes. It is recommended for building casinos, gambling-houses, pubs, clubs, factories, etc.

13

Shapes of Plots and Vaastu

L and is a blessing of nature for human beings, but not every shape of a plot of land is auspicious for residence. Generally square, rectangular and circular plots are considered good for constructing buildings.

Apart from the above mentioned shapes, plots of various other distinct shapes are described below with good or bad effects on the occupants of these plots.

Egg-shaped Plot: Residing in egg-shaped premises may cause anxiety, depression and plenty of other problems.

Triangular Plot: Those residing in a house constructed on a triangular plot are liable to face litigation and hazards of fire.

Semi-circular Plot: A house built on a semi-circular plot of land denies peace of mind and happiness to the people residing in it.

Octagonal Plot: An eight-sided plot of land is called an octagonal plot and a house constructed on such a plot is believed to give mental peace and prosperity to its residents.

Star shaped Plot: Constructions on a star shaped plot of land cause financial losses, litigation and confusion in life.

Fan-Shaped Plot: A fan shaped or *pankhakaar* plot of land resembles a hand held traditional Indian fan. Houses constructed on such plots may cause loss of money and domestic animals.

***Mridangakaar* Plot:** A *mridang* is an Indian traditional double sided drum used in *Kirtans,* etc. Living in houses built on such plots is not recommended at all as the residents may face extreme sufferings and sorrows.

Square-Shaped Plot: A square shaped plot is 90° from all four sides. It is considered an ideal plot for all types of construction whether it is commercial or residential.

Rectangular Plot: Rectangular plots are considered equally ideal as square-shaped plot. Rectangular plot in any directions i.e. along north-south length or along east-west length provides peace, prosperity and health.

Various Shapes of Plots

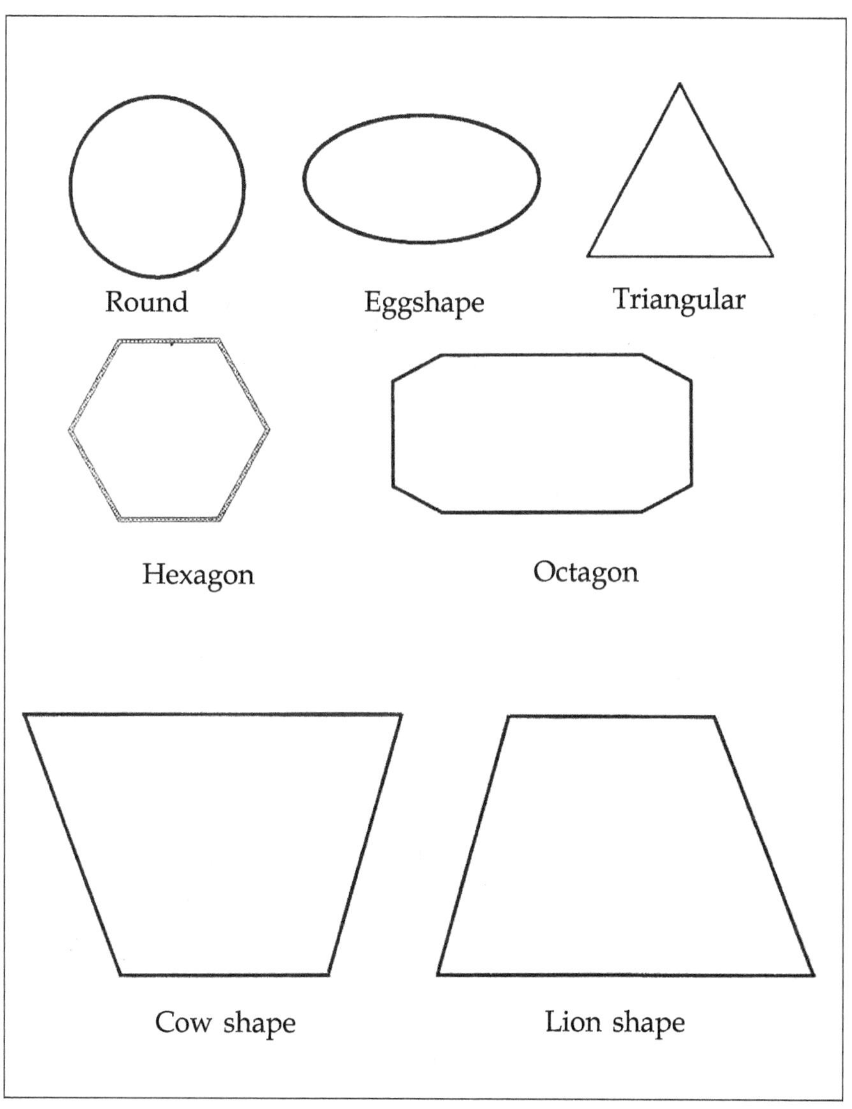

Plots with Extended or Torn Corners

The corners of a plot of land are crucial as these are the meeting points of two different directions. There are, however, also the plots with either extended or torn (cut) corners. These types may decrease or increase the auspiciousness of houses constructed there.

Extended North-east Corner

North-east is the meeting point of two very auspicious directions, viz. north and east. Because of the positive energy coming from the north and east, the north-east corner is most auspicious and there can be extensions as shown in Figure B 14.1 to Figure B 14.3

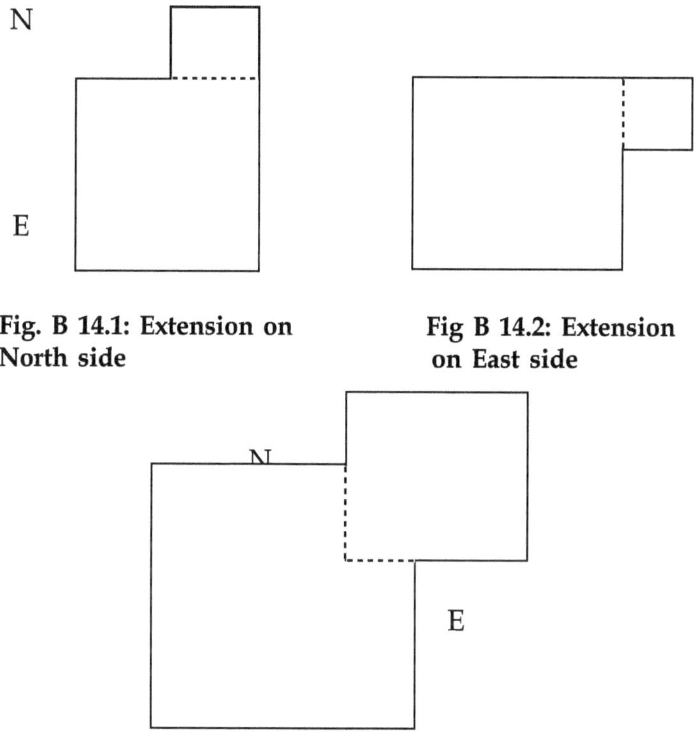

Fig. B 14.1: Extension on North side

Fig B 14.2: Extension on East side

Fig. B 14.3: Extended North-east Corner

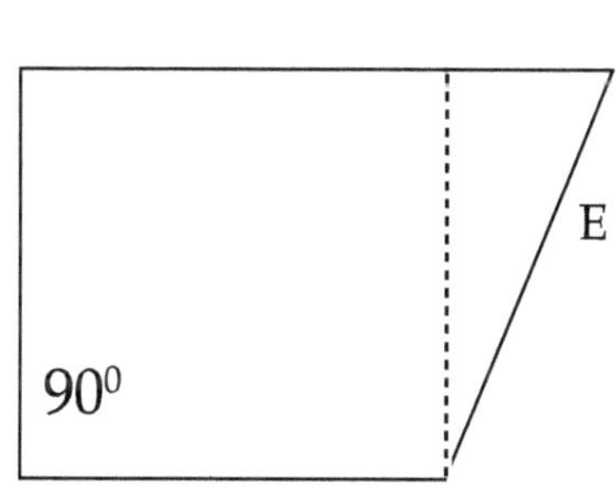

Fig. B 14.4 Inauspicious Extension

Any extension, which causes the corner to have an angle other than 90° such as the one shown in Figure B 14.4, is considered inauspicious.

As we know that the north-east corner is the place where the head of the vaastu purush resides and therefore extension of this corner is considered good. But if this corner is cut or torn then it is equally bad and inauspicious.

It is recommended that if a plot of land is not symmetrical or has torn or defaced corners then the plot should be made symmetrical before construction.

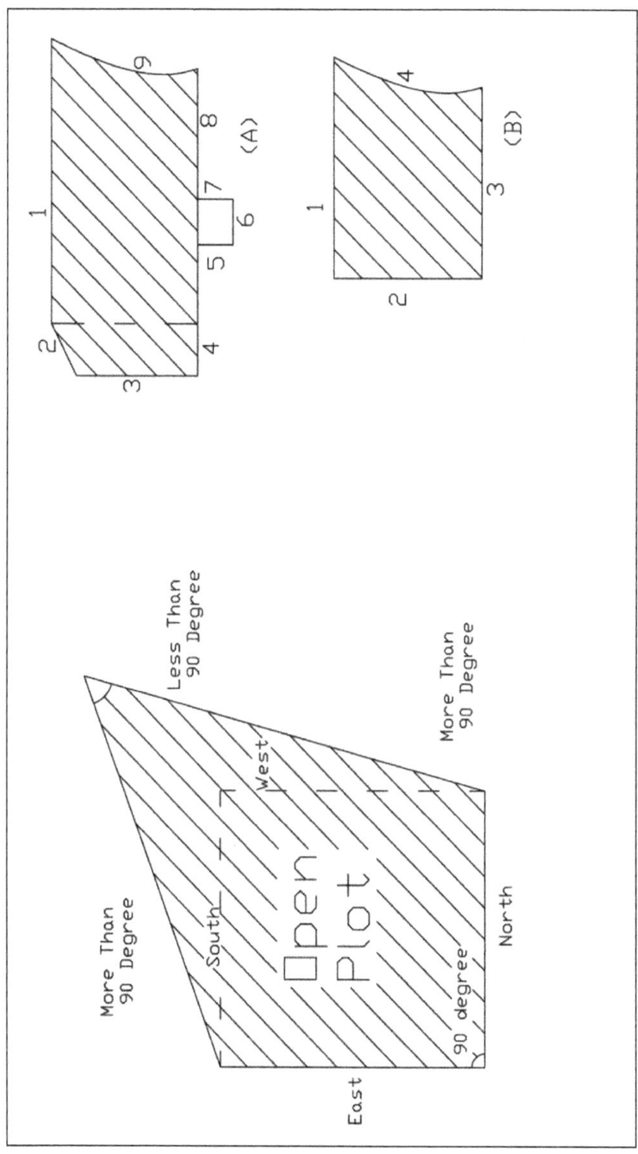

Extended plot in south-west (as shown in this figure) is not recommended as per vaastu. The above two figures shows how we can make the plot ideal by cutting extended portion.

Vaastu in Practice

Important Vaastu Mahuratas

In recent past renowned western scientist Albert Einstein investigated the nature of 'Time' and gave it a significant place in his 'Theory of Relativity'. But his approach, as is the case with all western scientists, was limited only to the physical phenomenon.

Our ancient wise sages with their supernatural powers uncovered even the metaphysical aspects of physical phenomenon. Suitable example is the science of mahurata or electing an auspicious time for beginning any important work.

Well begun is half done!

The Hindu philosophy propounds that the moment of commencement of anything carries the seed of success or failure of that work.

This chapter enumerates and analyses such mahuratas as well as prominent events or ceremonies related to *vaastu*. The occasions are:

1. Purchasing land for construction
2. Laying the foundation
3. Entering a new premises
4. Purchasing a built-up house
5. Shifting to another house
6. Repairing a house

An analytical description of the above follows below.

1. Purchasing land for construction

The most auspicious constellation (nakshatra), week days and lunar days *(Tithi)* for this event are indicated in the following Table:

Table C 15.1

Auspicious Constellations Nakshatras)	Favourable Weekdays	Lunar Dates (Tithis)
The following Nakshatras are considered auspicious for this ceremony: Ashvini, Rohini, Mrigshira, Punarvasu, Pushya, Hasta, Swati, Anuradha, Utraashadha, Shravana, Dhanishtha, Shatbhisha, Utrabhadrapad	The favourable weekdays are: Mondays, Wednesdays, Thursdays and Saturdays.	Avoid these lunar dates: 4th, 9th and 14th of a lunar month. These lunar dates are called *Rikta Tithis* and are not auspicious for this ceremony.

The **Mahurata Kundali:** When the day for this event has been finalised, an expert should be consulted to cast an astrological chart for the most favourable time of that day for the dealing. While doing so the following factors need attention:

The ascendant *(Lagna)* of the *Mahurata Kundali* has to be selected from any one of the signs -Taurus, Leo, Scorpio or Aquarius.

The planet jupiter should preferably occupy a square or a trine house, viz. the houses 1st, 4th, 5th, 7th, 9th or 10th. The planet Mars should preferably be in the 11th house but never in the ascendant.

The lord of the 11th house should not be positioned in the 12th house. It is advisable that the lords of the 1st and the 7th houses are well placed.

2. Laying the foundation

The foundation laying ceremony is of great importance as it decides the future of a building. Selecting a mahurata or auspicious time for this ceremony will ensure longevity and general good of the building.

Best lunar months for this ceremony: The Vaastu purusha is shown lying with his head in the northeast direction but it is not its permanent position and shifts according to the lunar months as given in the Table.

Table C 15.2: Direction of the head and vision (Drishti) of the *Vaastu Purush* during different periods of a year

Lunar Months	Direction of the Vaastu Purusha's Head and *Drishti*
Bhadrapad, Ashvin, Kartika	East
Margshirsh, Paush, Magha	South
Phalgun, Chaitra Vaishakh,	West
Jyeshtha, Ashadha, Shravan	North

The lunar months considered best for this ceremony are chaitra, vaishakh, shravan, kartika and magha.

While selecting a mahurata, the other factors marked as per the following Table C 15.3 must be heeded as well:

Table C 15.3

Auspicious Constellations (Nakshatras)	Favourable Weekdays	Lunar Dates (Tithis)	The Transit of the Sun
The following Nakshatras are considered auspicious for this ceremony: Rohini, Mrigshira, Chitra, Hasta, Jyeshtha, Utraashadha and Shravan.	The favourable weekdays are: Mondays, Wednesdays, Thursdays and Fridays are the most suitable but during the waning phase of the Moon Mondays are best avoided	The auspicious tithis are the 1st, 2nd, 3rd, 5th, 6th, 7th, 10th, 11th and 13th. All other tithis should be avoided.	The time when the Sun is transiting in dual signs, viz. Gemini, Virgo, Sagittarius and Pisces should be avoided. The best are the fixed signs, viz. Taurus, Leo, Scorpio and Aquarius. But if there is an emergency then even the movable signs viz. Aries, Cancer, Libra and Capricorn may also be considered.

Vaastu Kundali: While making a chart for selecting the most auspicious moment to commence this work, following should be taken into consideration:

The best signs falling in the ascendant are Taurus, Leo, Scorpio and Aquarius.

All malevolent planets should be in the 3rd, 6th and 11th houses and the benefices in the square and trine houses. The 8th house should preferably be vacant and free from any malevolent element.

3. Entering a New Premises

The lunar months of vaishakha, jyeshtha, magha and phalgun are most auspicious for this ceremony but in cases of emergency kartika and margshira can also be considered. The sun should be transiting in the northern hemisphere *(utrayan)*.

The most auspicious constellation (nakshatra), week days and lunar days *(tithi)* for this event are indicated in refer to the following Table:

Table C 15.4

Auspicious Constellations (Nakshatras)	Favourable Weekdays	Lunar Dates (Tithis)
The following nakshatras are considered auspicious for this ceremony: rohini, mrigshira, utraashadha, chitra and utrabhadrapad are the best. But if necessary, anuradha and revati can also be considered. Some consider the birth constellation of the native as most auspicious for this event.	The favourable weekdays are: Mondays, Wednesdays, Thursdays and Fridays	Only the 1st of the dark half and 2nd, 3rd, 5th, 7th, 10th, 11th and 13th of the bright half phase of the Moon are considered best for this occasion.

Mahurata chart: For the exact auspicious time for this event a chart is to be cast. The ascendant sign should be a fixed sign, viz. Taurus, Leo, Scorpio or Aquarius. The 8th house should be vacant and all malevolent planets in the 3rd, 6th, 10th and 11th houses.Entering a new house should be avoided if the wife of the owner is in the advanced stages of pregnancy.

4. Buying a built-up house

Many people prefer buying a built-up house. In that case, the deal could be struck according to the below Table:

Table C 15.5

Auspicious Constellations (Nakshatras)	Favourable Weekdays	Lunar Dates (Tithis)
The following nakshatras are considered auspicious for this ceremony: mrigshira, ashlesha, magha, vaishakha, moola, punarvasu and revati.	Thursdays and Fridays are best.	Nanda Tithis, viz. 1st, 6th and 11th are auspicious for this occasion.

In respect of casting a chart for the *mahurat* time and for this Taurus, Gemini, Leo, Libra and Scorpio signs are best for the ascendant (lagna). There should not be any malevolent planet in the 7th house and mars should not be in the ascendant.

5. Shifting to another house

In matter of shifting to another house, a suitable mahurata can be worked out by referring to the table below:

Table C 15.6

Auspicious Constellations (Nakshatras)	Favourable Weekdays	Lunar Dates (Tithis)
One's own birth constellation is considered best for this occasion.	Mondays, Wednesdays, Thursdays and Fridays are best.	The rikta tithis viz. the 4th, 9th and 14th of a lunar month should be avoided.

6. *Getting a house repaired*

Repairs and maintenance are essential requirements of every house. All repair work should be commenced on a favourable day and time as indicated below:

Table C 15.7

Auspicious Constellations (Nakshatras)	Favourable Weekdays	Transit of Mars
One's own birth constellation is considered best for this occasion.	If the Mahurata kundali has Taurus or Libra ascendant sign then fridays and if the Mahurata Kundali has Cancer ascendant sign then Mondays are the best times for commencing any repair work. If not so, just avoiding Tuesdays will suffice.	It is best to avoid starting repair work when Mars is transiting through any of the following constellations: kritika, magha, pushya, hasta, moola or revati.

In the mahurata kundali a benevolent planet should occupy the ascendant and the moon should be in the Cancer sign.

Planning According to Directions

t is a privilege owning a house. For some it is a dream come true. People toil for years to save enough money to buy a piece of land and then put in more efforts to construct a house there.

Every one wishes to have a house which gives peace, health and prosperity to all the members of the family. However, if moving to a new house brings troubles, diseases and poverty then one's dreams are shattered.

Following the vaastu principles ensures progress accompanied by peace, happiness and harmony.

It is advisable to construct a room in the north-east corner for worship, meditation, spiritual and general studies.

A room adjoining the north wall of the plot may be used as children's bedroom. The drawing or sitting room is best located in the north-west corner.

The bedroom for the head of the house is also known as the master room and south-west is the best location for this. Toilet is best located along the south wall of the plot and kitchen in the south-east corner. Bathrooms are best located along the east wall.

The central portion of the plot, also called the brahmasthan is best left empty, or at least it should be kept clean and tidy.

If the above given suggestions are followed by consulting an expert on vaastu before planning construction then you can expect to own an ideal house.

Roads on the Sides of the Plot

Another important consideration is the roads alongside a plot. The adjoining roads play an important role in determining the auspiciousness of a plot.

In this context, there could be the following four situations:

Roads on all four sides: In case there are roads on all the four sides of a plot, it is considered auspicious. Such plots can be used for residential as well as commercial purposes.

Roads on three sides: If there are adjoining roads along the north, east and west sides of the plot but none along the south side, such a plot is not recommended for residential purposes. It can be good for commercial purposes provided that there is a door in the east or west side.

Roads on two sides: A plot with roads on its north and east sides is good for residential as well as commercial purposes. Such a place is also called an *Eeshaan* place and promises progress and prosperity.

A plot with roads on east and south sides is known as Aagneye place and is also considered auspicious.

A plot with roads on south and west sides is called nairitya place and is recommended for residential as well as commercial purposes.

A plot with roads on its north and west sides is called vayavya place and is good only for residential purposes.

If there are roads on north and south sides, the entrance must be on the north side.

A plot with roads on east and west sides is good only for commercial purposes.

Road on one side only: A road on north side is considered very auspicious for residential as well as commercial buildings. A plot with a road on its east side comes at the second place in auspiciousness for both residential and commercial purposes. A road on west side is also good for both purposes. But a plot with road on its south side is good for commercial purposes only.

Corner Plots

Many people like to have a corner plot mainly because it has more open space along the plot where one can have a garden. Vaastu recommends corner plots having open space on its north and east sides. Plots with open spaces along other directions are not considered auspicious.

The following table is helpful in this regard:

Table C 16.1: Directions in which open spaces exist, their negative effects and remedial measures

Open Spaces Towards	Negative Effects	Remedy
North and West	Negative thoughts and danger of getting addicted to something.	Building the west side compound wall as thick and high as feasible.
East and South	Financial problems and mental tension	Increasing the height and thickness of the south boundary wall.
South and West	Inauspicious for the family head and his or her eldest son.	Increasing the height and thickness of south and west boundary walls

First Floor

A construction on the first floor of a house must be on the south-west side above the ground floor construction. The balcony should be in the north or east and terrace on its left side.

The bedroom or study room for the head of the house should be situated on the first floor. Its windows and doors should be on north or east side. A large window on northwest side is preferable.

The roof height of the first floor must not be more than that of the ground floor. The slope of the first floor should be towards north or east side. The system for rain water drainage is best provided in the north, east or north-east.

A balcony in the southwest corner is strictly prohibited and also it should not be round or irregular in shape.

Auspicious Symbols and Tools in Vaastu

We all wish for good things. Depending upon their faith and beliefs people try different things and ways which are supposed to attract good luck, and one of these is the use of auspicious symbols. There are many symbols considered auspicious which can be used in premises. Also there are some tools and instruments which are used in vaastu practice and one must know about these. This chapter attempts to describe both symbols and tools.

Auspicious Symbols

This subhead deals with some auspicious symbols, namely 1. Om, 2. Swastik, 3. Mangal Kalash, 4. Panchasulak (Open hand impression representing the five elements), and 5. Meen (Fish)

Om: Om is believed to symbolise Brahma, the creator. The whole cosmos is contained in this word. This sacred word uttered correctly with faith produces peace of mind. This sacred symbol inscribed in any premises bestows divine blessings.

Swastik: The use of this most sacred symbol goes back to ancient times. In order to counter any kind of vaastu dosha (defect) in a premise, a swastik pyramid is fixed on each side of the main door.

A swastik sign inscribed on the ledger and cash box (*Tijori*) enhances the business and brings prosperity.

Mangal kalash (auspicious pot): Mangal kalash is also an integral part of Indian tradition seeking good luck through auspicious symbols. It is an earthen pot filled with pure water and decorated with mango or *Ashoka* leaves, *mouli* (sacred red thread), etc. and worshipped. It is believed to attract prosperity and well-being. This is essential to all auspicious ceremonies.

It is used at the time of entry into a new house (*Grihparvesh*) and is considered very auspicious.

Panchasulak: It is an open hand impression representing the five elements. Everything around and also our bodies are made out of these elements which signifies the use of this symbol for good luck. It enjoys immense religious significance in Jainism.

Hindus put an impression of palms smeared with turmeric paste on the occasion of *grihaparvesh*, birth ceremony, marriage ceremonies, etc.

A panchasulak impression put on the main entrance attracts prosperity, happiness and overall good and well-being.

Some other holy symbols and phrase are used by people of various religions for auspicious beginnings or harmony.

Sikhs

Jainism

Meen (Fish): The fish is traditionally linked with prosperity. A symbol showing a pair of fish promotes love. A symbol or image of fish in the north direction increases prosperity.

Placing a fish aquarium in recommended direction is believed to bring good luck. Before going out of the house viewing a fish is considered good. If a fish in the aquarium dies a natural death, it is said to take away the negative energy of the premises.

Tools and Instruments

For vaastu practice, the two basic items required are a measuring tape and a magnetic compass.

Measuring Tape: A measuring tape helps in various measurements in the premises and particularly in determining a suitable auspicious place for locating the main entrance, etc. A flexible and foldable measuring tape of at least ten meters length is ideal.

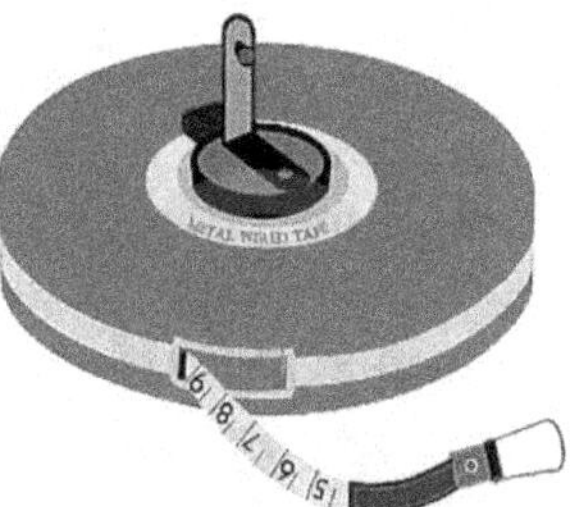

Magnetic Compass: A magnetic compass is used to determine the directions in the premises. A magnetic compass for vaastu purpose has to be of a reasonably good quality. The general appearance of a magnetic compass may vary from one make to another. One such type is shown in this Figure.

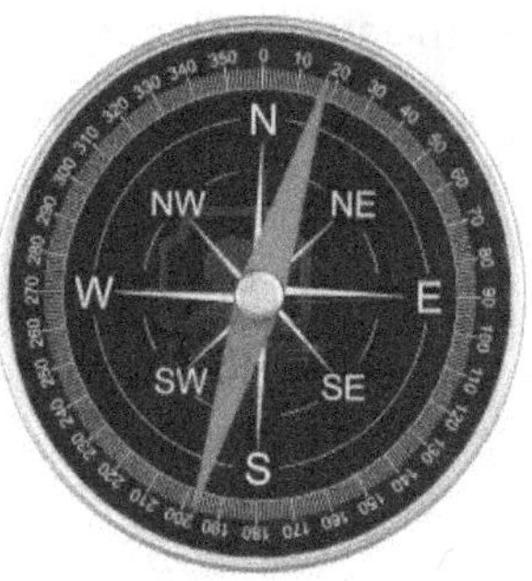

Fig C 17.1: A good quality magnetic compass with directions and 0° to 360° markings on the dial.

A magnetic arm usually called a needle with two pointed ends is suspended on a vertical pivot point. This arm or needle moves freely and if the compass is placed flat on a non-magnetic surface, its needle settles on the north-south axis of the earth. The end pointing towards the geographic north pole of the earth is usually painted red.

After the needle becomes stationary, the compass is slowly rotated in order to align the pointed end on the letter N (North) on its dial. Thus the compass is aligned and one can read the direction of any place.

To determine the directional location of anything in the premises, the map or plan of the premises is spread on a wooden surface or floor. One must keep away all magnetic materials such as iron. On any professional map there is an indication of the direction usually with an arrow pointing north.

The compass is placed on this and rotated so that the red marked end of compass needle is aligned with the North (N) mark on the compass dial. Then the compass should be slightly lifted and the map so aligned that the north pointing arrow indication on it is also aligned on the north marking on the compass dial. Now the exact directional location of any room or place in the premises can be easily determined.

18

Importance of Adjoining Plots

How auspicious is the plot of a land purchased by you for residential or commercial use depends upon various factors like type of soil, shape of plot, its corners, its directional alignment and the general environment and adjoining plots among others.

Vaastu does not recommend a plot near cremation or burial ground, slaughter house, memorials, etc. Such surroundings impede the progress and prosperity of dwellers.

In case there are trees like peepal, bargad and goolar near a plot with their roots reaching underneath it then also it is proclaimed inauspicious.

A plot at the end of a closed street is also considered inauspicious.

It is therefore advised essential that before purchasing a plot one must examine its adjoining areas. The following information could be quite useful in this regard. Buying an auspicious plot adjoining yours considering the following suggestions can boost the auspiciousness of one's first plot also:

1. If there is a plot available in the north-east of one's existing plot then it should be purchased immediately whatever may be the cost. An investment in such a plot can bring immense prosperity.

2. A plot near the southeast corner of your existing plot is also good.

3. A plot in the north or east direction beyond your plot's northeast corner is very auspicious and gives financial benefits.

4. One should never buy a plot in the north of their existing plot's north-west corner as it tends to increase the north-west side of their plot and thus causes loss in business.

5. One should never buy a plot adjoining their plot's south-east, south-west corners even if it is very cheap. Such plots spell theft and bad luck.

6. Vaastu does not recommend purchasing or taking on rent a plot in the south or west side of an existing plot.

7. If an adjoining flat or house touches the upper side of one's house and it is constructed as per vaastu principles it can be purchased safely.

8. Purchasing an adjoining plot or house in the east of one's house is auspicious if there is a river or a canal in the north or east of that adjoining plot.

19

The Main Entrance

The Vaastu Shastra suggests eight possible places in each direction of a plot of land for locating the main entrance also called *mukhya dwara, mukhya* meaning ' main' and *dwara* meaning a 'door'. As there are four sides of a plot there is a possibility of 32 main entrances as shown in Figure C 5.1.

Whether an entrance at a particular location is good or bad is decided by the nature of the *devta* (deity) governing that place.

The main entrance in a building is very important as it links the building and its inhabitants with the outside world. As the occupants of a house go out through that door for performing various jobs and expect success, the main door has to be suitably located to grant them success and fulfilment of their dreams. After performing their work, people come back and enter the premises expecting peace and harmony.

North

Roga 25	Naag 26	Mukhya 27	Bhalaat 28	Soma 29	Bhujag 30	Aaditi 31	Diti 32	Shikhi 1
Paapyak-shama 24								Parjanye 2
Shosh 23								Jayant 3
Asur 22								Indra 4
Varun 21								Surya 5
Pushpd-ant 20								Satya 6
Sugreev 19								Bhrish 7
Dovaarik 18								Antriksh 8
Pitar 17	Mrig 16	Bhringraj 15	Gandharv 14	Yam 13	Brihitkshat 12	Vitath 11	Poosha 10	Anil 9

South

Fig. C 19.1: The diagram shows in all 32 possible places, on an 81 cell plan, for locating the main entrance or door.

The nature of main entrance

To determine the nature of an entrance at a particular place in all the four directions of a plot, we refer again to the chapter titled 'Vastuvidyadhyaya' of *Brihat Samhita* by Acharya Varah Mihir.

The shloka 69 of this chapter says:

'Navgunsootrvibhaktanyeashtgunonathva chatushashtey,

dwarani yani teshamanladinaam phalopanye.'

The above shloka infers that in the 81-cell vaastu chakra there are 9 cells in each direction but in 64-step vaastu chakra there are 8 cells. However in both cases there can be a maximum of 8 doors in one direction so in all four directions there can be 32 doors. We will now describe the nature of each entrance.

Nature of the east side entrances:

Shloka 70 of the above chapter is quoted below:

'Aniolbhayam istrijannam prabhotdhanta narendarvaalabhayam,

krodhpartanrittvam karoriyam choriyam cha poorven.'

The nature of all entrances on this side as described in this shloka are in Table given below.

Table C 19.1: East side Entrances and their Nature

Governing Deity	Practical nature of entrance
Shikhi	Danger of Fire
Parjanya	Birth of daughters
Jayant	Immense wealth
Indra	Favour of king or ruler or authorities in general
Surya	Tendency to cause flared tempers
Satya	Tendency to cheat and tell lies
Bhrish	Cruelty
Antriksh	Theft

Note: Some people believe that the entrance at the place governed by surya is good and gives wealth. According to others it leads to bad temper.

Nature of the South Side Entrances

Shloka 71 of the same chapter as quoted below explains the south side entrances and their nature.

'Alpsuttwam preshyam neechatvam bhakshaipaansutvridhi,

roudrumkritghanmadhnamsutveeryedhanam cha yamyen.'

Table C 19.2: South Side Entrances and their Nature

Governing Deity	Practical nature of entrance
Anil	Very few progeny
Poosha	Gives feeling of subservience
Vitath	Low grade work and behaviour
Brihitkshat	Plenty to eat and birth of male progeny.
Yam	Inauspicious
Gandharv	Tendency to be ungrateful
Bhringraj	Gives poverty
Mrig	Loss of son's prowess

Note: Some people believe that the entrance at the place ruled by Yam gives wealth and that ruled by Gandharv gives fearlessness and fame.

Nature of the West Side Entrances

Shloka 72 of the same chapter as given below explains the west side entrances and their nature.

'Sutpeeda ripuvridhir nai sutdhunapti sutarthphalsampat,

dhansampanniptibhayam dhankshyo rog ityepare.'

The results denoted in this shloka are given below in Table.

Table C 19.3: West Side Entrances and their Nature

Governing Deity	Practical nature of entrance
Pitr	Suffering by children
Dowarik	Increase of enemies
Sugreev	Progeny and wealth
Pushpdant	Progeny and wealth
Varun	Wealth
Asur	Fear of the ruler or authorities
Shosh	Loss of wealth
Paapyakshama	Diseases

Nature of the North Side Entrances:

Shloka 73 of the same chapter explains the north side entrances and their nature.

'Vadhbandho ripuvridhi sutdhanlabhai smastgunsampat,

putrdhanpatirvairum sutein dosha istriya naishawam'

The results denoted in this shloka are as given in the table below:

Table C 19.4: North Side Entrances and their Nature

Governing Deity	Practical nature of entrance
Rog	Death or bondage
Naag	Increase of enemies
Mukhya	Progeny and wealth
Bhalaat	Good qualities and wealth
Som	Increase of wealth and progeny
Bhujag	Enmity with son
Aditi	Suffering due to women
Diti	Poverty

The points to ponder while planning the main entrance:

1. The main entrance should be larger than all other doors in the house.
2. The height of the main door should be double its width.
3. The main door must not close and open on its own.
4. There should not be any door in the middle part of the house as it is believed to cause poverty and quarrels.
5. The main door should be rectangular in shape or semi circular on top. A triangular shape door is prohibited.
6. A main door slanting inside is bad for the head of the family and one slanting outward causes displacement.
7. The doors must not open outwards.
8. A staircase opposite the main door is best avoided.
9. Each side of the main door should be adequately lit.
10. Decorating the main door is not advisable; this may attract evil-eye *(buri-nazar)*.
11. The main door should not be painted black.
12. It is auspicious to keep potted plants near the main entrance.
13. Auspicious symbols or their pictures such as swastika, Ganpati (Lord Ganesha), gold coins, cow with a calf or any picture depicting motherly love are recommended at the entrance.

The Brahmasthan

The central portion of a premise is called the *Brahmasthan*. This space bears a special import in vaastu and should not be overlooked while planning a house.

How to locate the Brahmasthan?

We have seen in the Figure B 8.1 of chapter 8 of section B that in an 81 cell residential vaastu chakra the central 9 cells define the brahmasthan.

Figure below highlights this central place as the shaded portion.

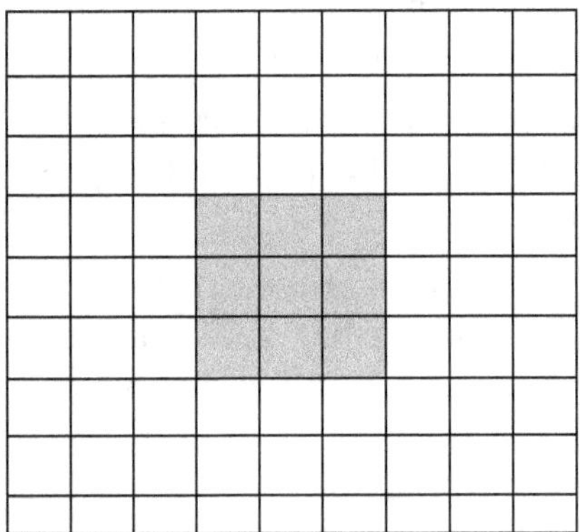

Fig. C 20.1: The shaded central portion is called *Brahmasthan*

Importance of Brahmasthan

The stomach of the vaastu purush covers this central portion. The importance of stomach in any body for keeping good health is nothing abstruse. As one cannot fill one's stomach with junk food items if keeping good health is the consideration, so in a premise the Brahmasthan has to be clutter-free. This area of the house should be kept clean and tidy and free of junk items. Taking care of this improves the overall auspiciousness of the premises.

The ancient vaastu treatises recommend construction of a temple of the family deity at this place.

In Rajasthan it was a common practice to keep this space well lit and covered, from where one could go in all rooms or areas of the house. A potted basil plant and idol of some deity was kept here.

Common vaastu doshaas (defects) and suggested remedial measures

1. If the brahmasthan is unclean and filled with junk or discarded items, the occupants may suffer ill health. A toilet, underground water tank, septic tank, borewell, etc. in this area is strictly prohibited as this causes troubles and lack of peace.
2. In case of absence of natural light artificial lights can be fixed in this area.
3. The walls or doors in this area should be painted white. Also, use white curtains if necessary.
4. Keeping a potted basil plant in this place will fill it with positive vibrations.
5. For plots of odd shapes it may be difficult to exactly mark the brahmasthan. Strategic placement of vaastu pyramids after consulting a vaastu expert can cure such defects.
6. If the brahmasthan on the ground floor is kept empty then on the first floor the side walls of this portion should be about one or two feet higher than the floor level. Provision for proper ventilation and day light is

a must. In case the brahmasthan has to be covered, the roof should be in pyramid shape or with a slant towards north or east and thick glass or clear fibre sheets have to be placed here to allow the sunlight inside.

Basement

Generally vaastu shastra does not recommend a basement because sun rays do not reach there. However a basement with its one fourth areas higher than the plot level allowing entry of sunrays between 7am and 10am is feasible. In Western countries a large mirror is fixed to reflect sunrays into the basement.

A basement is not recommended for living purposes particularly for a sick person as it diminishes the chances of their recovery.

North and east are the best directions for a basement with windows and doors in the north and east side. A basement in south and west direction is not advised. And, there should be no heavy things in the south-west part of the basement.

Commercial activities can be done in the north-west part of the basement but there is a danger of sudden loss. A basement is best used for storage only.

There should not be a borewell or water supply in the southwest of a basement as this causes danger of accidents or suicidal tendencies for the owner.

A hotel in the southeast part of a basement is good but its kitchen must fulfill vaastu requirements.

A temple in the basement increases occult power of the worshippers as it is filled with positive magnetic energy. In case a commercial activity is operated from a basement then the cash counter, cash box, etc. must be kept at the ground floor and not in the basement.

If due to limitation of space a basement is necessary then the important points mentioned above must be acted upon in order to avoid serious vaastu defects.

Bathroom

According to vaastu the best location for bathroom is in the east. An east facing window in the bathroom is ideal for entry of morning sunrays for health and positive vibrations. The bathroom door is always good towards north or east but never in the south.

The floor of the bathroom must be sloping towards north or east so that water flows towards these directions and drains out. A mirror on the north or east wall attracts good luck.

A Bath tub if any is best located in the west part and along the north-south axis so that the head of the person lying in the bed should be towards south.

A water heater (geyser) and all other electrical equipment are advisably fixed in the south-east corner of bathroom.

The shower and wash basin should either be in the north-east or east direction.

Clothes should be washed in the north-west corner of the bathroom.

Common vaastu doshaas (defects) and suggested remedial measures

1. To get over minor vaastu defects of a bathroom, the bather should face east.

2. The walls of the bathroom must be painted white, light-pink, light-blue or in pastel shades for removing any vaastu defects.

3. Vaastu does not recommend combining toilet with bathroom but if it does exist then the toilet seat must be so located that a person while sitting on it faces south.

23

Bedroom

Bedroom is a very personal and important part of a house. Bedroom is a place where one relaxes and enjoys a restful sleep. If in spite of all comforts one does not feel relaxed and calm, it could be due to some vaastu defect in the bedroom. In a house depending upon the space available there can be separate bedrooms for different members. No bedroom should be located in the north-east direction as such a bedroom hinders the progress of the family.

Some essential vaastu principles as given below should be followed in all bedrooms:

1. The bed in any bedroom should be so placed that while sleeping one's feet are not in front of a door.

2. While sleeping no part of one's body should be visible in a mirror placed in that room, this may cause bad dreams and bodyache.

3. One should never sleep naked in a bedroom.

4. In a bedroom, one should never sleep under a beam.

5. Bed should be so placed that while sleeping the head of a person is towards south and never towards north.

6. A black or red coloured bed sheet or curtains are never good in a bedroom. Light and cool colours should be preferred.

7. One should never place any water body like a fish aquarium or a fountain in a bedroom.

8. A temple in a bedroom is best avoided.

9. Wardrobe should be located in south or west direction.

10. Refrigerator, air conditioner and television should be placed in south-east corner.

11. The best direction for windows in a bedroom is the north or east.

12. A bedroom should be decorated with natural or artificial flowers.

Master Bedroom

A master bedroom is the bedroom for the head of the family. This room can be used by the head of the family or his or her eldest son.

In a multi-storey house this bedroom should be at the topmost floor and bigger than all other bedrooms.

The ideal location for this room is in the south-west direction of the plot.

Bedrooms for Others

Bedroom for adult members can be built in south or west direction. Bedroom for students and young children should be in the southeast. Bedroom for girls of marriageable age is best located in northwest.

In the bedroom for a married couple, the pictures of love scenes like two birds caressing each other should be placed in the south-west direction.

24

Boring for Water

Nowadays a lot of people prefer a boring well in the premises in order to cope with the general shortage of water supply in many cities.

For boring, digging a well or underground water tanks, etc. vaastu recommends the north side of the diagonal line joining north-east and south-west corners of the plot.

Boring can be started soon after the worship ceremony of the new plot of land.

Common vaastu doshaas (defects) and suggested remedial measures

1. A boring or underground water storage in the west or north-west direction spells danger of cancer in the stomach.

2. By locating any underground water source in the west or north side of the north-west direction one runs into the danger of poverty and tensions among the family members due to that.

3. If in a premises the underground water sources such as a borewell, underground water storage tank or a well exist in the west or north-west direction then by placing pyramid yantras in these directions one can minimise the negative effects of vaastu defects.

25

Children's Room

Children need right kind of environment for their overall development. In this regard care and close attention of parents and a right kind of atmosphere at school is essential.

Vaastu plays a crucial role towards children's development and progress in life.

A child needs a separate room for a right kind of atmosphere. Children's room is best located in the north, east, north-east or the north-west directions.

If due to some reason it is not possible to have the children's room in the above directions then one may consider the southeast but never the south or southwest.

Place the bed along the east-west axis. The study table should be so placed that the child faces east while studying.

Common vaastu doshaas (defects) and suggested remedial measures

The children's room must be free of any vaastu defect resulting from its wrong location. If such a defect exists, the following measures may be adopted to minimise the negative effects:

1. Fixing energised sun yantra on the east wall and budh yantra on the north wall of the room. The sun yantra will lift up the morale and the budh (mercury) yantra will increase concentration and interest in studies.

2. Painting the walls of the room with light shades of cool colours like green or blue or cream and hanging curtains of such colours.

3. Hanging beautiful sceneries on the walls and placing flowers in a vase.

26

Dining Room

A dining room adjacent to a toilet creates vaastu defects. There are different views about the best location for a dining room but as far as the author's opinion is considered, the west direction is the most appropriate. In view of space limitations, one can have a dining room in the east or north. The door of this room should be either in north or east direction and never in the south direction.

The sitting arrangement should be such that while taking food the head of the family faces east while other members may face east, north or west but never south as that reduces mutual love and attachment.

Provision for drinking water should be in the north-east and wash basin in north or east and never in southeast or northwest.

The door of the dining room should not face the main door of the house.

Common vaastu doshaas (defects) and suggested remedial measures

In general the ambience of the dining room or dining area should be pleasing and calm. Use of proper colours and furnishing can perk up your appetite and help in digestion. By incorporating the following measures one can minimise the negative effects of vaastu doshas and enhance the positive vibrations of the area:

1. Using cream, orange and pink to paint the walls and for the curtains.

2. Avoiding a cluttered and untidy dining area as it reduces appetite and proper assimilation of food.

3. One or two (depending upon the space available) potted green leafy plants such as *maansarovar* to fill the area with positive energy.

4. If possible one should keep a round dining table instead of any other shape and three or five chairs instead of four. A round chair improves communication among family members.

27

Drawing Room

A drawing room is used as a meeting place for family members and for receiving the guests and visitors. Apart from its vaastu compatibility the drawing room should be furnished to reflect one's style of living and social status. If possible the drawing room should be big enough to accommodate at least eight or ten guests.

If the drawing room fails to comfort and impress the visitors then it must be under some vaastu doshas.

The best directions for building a drawing or living room are north, east or northeast avoiding the diagonal energy lines of the plot.

The door can be preferably on the east side near the north-east corner avoiding the diagonal energy lines.

Common vaastu doshaas (defects) and suggested remedial measures

The following suggestions if followed sincerely can minimise the negative effects of vaastu doshas and harmonise the area.

1. Arranging the furniture in such a way that the central part of this room is kept vacant or very lightly furnished.

2. Using light shades of blue, green, yellow and white colours for painting its walls and curtains.

3. The family head should sit facing north or east directions and the guests facing south or west.

4. Small potted indoor plants may be kept in the north side but the larger or heavier ones need to be placed in the south or west.

5. Hanging a picture of the family deity in the northeast corner. Hanging a wind chime is also good. Hanging a mirror in this room is not advised.

6. Avoiding an 'L' shape sofa set. The centre table can be round, square or rectangular in shape. Prefer glass showcases instead of wooden ones. It is best to keep fish-aquarium, fountains, etc. in the north-east direction.

28

Electric Meter and Equipment

Next in importance to the northeast is the southeast corner and it should be kept free from vaastu defects. This direction is the abode of fire (Agni) element and therefore all electrically operated equipment as well as the electric meter and power control and distribution of the house should be located here. Doing so will keep the fire element under balance.

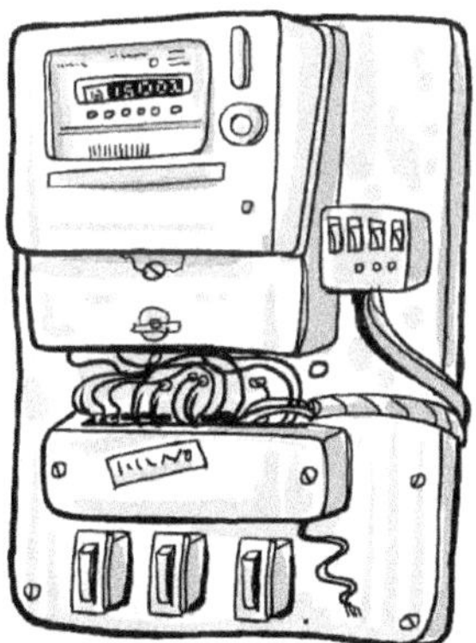

Common vaastu doshaas (defects) and suggested remedial measures

In case one happens to live in a house affected by vaastu doshas due to wrong use of south-east direction then the following suggestions will help in reducing the negative effects:

1. Imbalance of the fire element can cause health, marital and financial problems to the family members. These dangers are reduced by appeasement of the fire element by lighting a lamp (deepak) using mustard oil in the south-east corner.

2. Sit at the south-east corner and recite the Gayatri mantra at sunrise.

3. Vaastu defect existing in the southeast corner of the house can be minimised by taking care of this direction in every room of the house. Keeping washing machine, refrigerator, etc. in the south-east corner is an effective measure.

29

Garage

Vaastu suggests the north-west as the best direction for building a garage. In case north-west is not feasible it can be located in the south-east but never in the north-east or south-west.

It is recommended to have the garage separate from the main building of the house and not touching it.

One can build a parking in a low height basement for which north-west or east are the best directions.

The door of the garage should be in the east or north-west and its gate should be lower in height than the boundary wall.

Common vaastu doshaas (defects) and suggested remedial measures

The following measures will minimise the negative effects of the vaastu defects due to wrongly located garage:

1. If the garage is in the north-east, a servant room beside or above the garage is prohibited.
2. If the garage is in the north-west, the car should be parked facing east.
3. If the garage is in the south-east, the car should be facing north.

Guard Room

The best place for a guard room is outside the main entrance and on its left. The roof level should be low with windows on all sides.

In a house in where the guard room is at a wrong place and due to the negative effects of the vaastu doshas the guard is careless and does not do his job well, fixing mangal yantra on the south wall of the guard room will do the trick.

Guest Room

ndian culture and tradition equates a guest with god (devta) as the commonly used phrase, '*Atithi devo-bhava*' implies. It is unbound Indian compassion which gives so much respect to a visitor or a guest. In days gone by when life moved at a slow pace and everyone had plenty of time to spare, a guest could stay as long as desired. But no one these days would like a guest prolonging his or her stay unnecessarily. In this context, the science of vaastu suggests the north-west as the most appropriate direction for a guest house.

Being ruled by unsteady planet moon the north-west direction lacks stability and is linked to change and therefore any person living there should not be allowed to stay longer.

If a guest room in the north-west is not possible one may consider the south-east but never south-west. South-west belongs to the earth element and hence linked to stability.

Common vaastu doshaas (defects) and suggested remedial measures

The following suggestions, if sincerely followed, can minimise the negative effects of vaastu defects in a guest room:

1. A water fountain should be placed in the west side of the guest room.
2. Using light shades of green or blue for painting the walls. Hanging curtains of such light and cool shades will also help.
3. Excessively luxurious furnishings are not advised, but basic facilities for a comfortable stay are recommended.

Jumble Room

A jumble or junk room is normally not planned while constructing a house but becomes essential later on. In course of time junk items or *kabaad* accumulates in almost every house and one finds no place to keep it till it is disposed.

The recommended direction for a jumble room is south-west. This can be built in the south-west of the master bedroom and should be small in size.

The door of the jumble room should not be in south-east, north-east or south direction. This room should not have any window but if necessary it should be on the west wall.

This room should neither be lent out nor used for living by any member of the family otherwise that person will create problems for the head of the family and quarrel with other members.

Kitchen

A kitchen is an essentially important part of every household. It not only satisfies our taste buds but also provides food for sustenance.

One can say that a kitchen reflects a family's health and prosperity and the housewife's culinary skills.

As a housewife spends appreciable time in kitchen, it should be largely free from any vaastu defects in its environment so that everyone is benefited.

Vaastu recommends a kitchen in the south-east corner of the house as there is plenty of sunlight which kills bacteria. South-east corner belongs to the fire element and is governed by the planet Venus.

If building a kitchen in the south-east is not possible then it can be located in the east or south. Slope of the kitchen floor should be such that water drains out through north or east direction and never through south.

One should never build a kitchen in the north, north-east or south-west direction as this may create vaastu doshas.

As it is customary to cook in a standing position, a two feet wide platform with three feet height and length is recommended subject to availability of space. It is better to top the platform with white marble which absorbs heat.

In case a kitchen exists in a wrong place in a house, the vaastu dosha effects can be minimised by the following precautions:

- Water tap, wash basin, etc. should be in the north or north-east, cupboards in the south or west, refrigerator in south-west and cooking gas and burners in the south-east.
- The cooking burners should be so placed that the cook faces east while cooking.
- Facilities for ventilation and fresh air should be fixed on east and west walls. The doors should have wire net so that plenty of air and light can enter. The exhaust fan and chimney should be on east side.

Overhead Water Tank

Location of the overhead water tank is very important from the perspective of vaastu as placing it in the wrong direction can create serious problems.

Vaastu recommends placing the overhead water tank on the west side of the diagonal line joining the south-west and north-east corners of a plot.

The water tank must never be placed on the right of this diagonal line as it is a strategic and sensitive energy line of the plot of land. The tank can be located clear of this line and on its west side near the south-west corner. The tank should be on a base made with bricks and about nine inches in height.

It is unwise locating the overhead water tank in the central portion of the plot as this causes instability in life and the family finds it difficult to stay together.

An overhead tank placed in the north-east can cause health and financial problems and if it is located in the south-east it can cause serious financial problems as well as dangers of accident and litigation also mount.

Pet Animals

Vaastu shastra commands that the pet animals should not be kept inside the main building of a house. They can be kept in shelters or cages which are located outside the main building near the north-west corner and clear of the northern wall.

Keeping the pets inside the main building of the house drains away the positive energy of the area. This positive energy is essential for peace, progress and well-being of the human beings living in that house.

Pigeons, parrots and eagles are strictly prohibited from being kept inside the main building as they cause larger drainage of the positive energy.

36

Prayer Room

A small prayer or worship room is quite common in Indian houses.

North-east and the brahmasthan (central portion) are two ideal places for building a prayer room. One should never build a toilet under or above a prayer room.

Sometimes due to constraint of space a separate prayer room is not possible. Some people set a praying area inside the bedroom but generally it is not recommended because of a different atmosphere inside a bedroom. The best alternative is to make a wooden or cemented partition and set it as a prayer room.

The roof of the prayer room should preferably be shaped as a pyramid which energises the space underneath.

The idol or picture of the deity should be placed on the east side facing west. One should never keep a damaged picture or idol in the prayer room.

A prayer room should have a big window on its east wall allowing entry of daylight and morning sunrays. White or light blue shades are recommended for painting the walls or for curtains.

In a prayer room, one should never hang pictures of family members who have died.

The prayer room or the praying area should always be kept clean and tidy.

37

Servant Room

For a servant room the recommended direction is northwest. A servant's room in the south-west direction may be disastrous as this direction is meant for the owner or head of the family. A servant living in south-west will become dominant.

It is customary to construct a room for the servant on the first floor of a garage, but this should be avoided if the garage is in northeast or southwest.

If light things are kept on the north and east side in a servant's room, the servant remains faithful to the owner.

Staircase

A staircase is quite a common and an integral part of almost all houses and buildings. A staircase is needed for safely reaching other floors from the ground floor. Even in single storey houses, staircase may exist just for reaching the rooftop.

Notably the 'stairs not only take us up they take us down as well'. This is not just a general factual statement, but a great truth is hidden behind these words. Going by Vaastu, a person's rise and fall in life is linked with the staircase in that person's house. Thus it is of utmost importance to select the right location for a staircase.

The science of vaastu says that if the staircase in one's house is properly located in keeping with the vaastu guidelines then one is saved from multiple problems and instability in life.

The ideal place for constructing a staircase according to vaastu is south-west and west and south of south-west corner. The recommended area for a staircase is shown shaded in Figure.

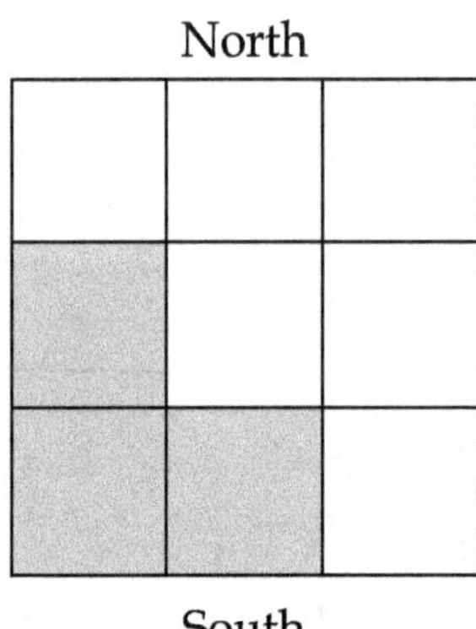

Fig. C 38: Area (shown shaded) recommended by Vaastu for locating a staircase.

The following suggestions if followed can bring progress, peace and harmony in one's life and household:

* The steps of the staircase should begin either from the north or east direction.

* Only if absolutely necessary one can locate stairs in the south-east or north-west direction also.

* Stairs opposite the main entrance are not recommended.

* Staircases in the northeast and brahmasthan are not considered auspicious and create serious vaastu dosha.

* Stairs should turn in the clockwise direction and the upper most step should be either in the south or west direction.

* One should use decorative but not slippery stones or tiles on the steps.
* A railing of some beautiful design on sides of the staircase is permissible.
* One should never make stairs in the northeast as this can cause financial and business losses and increase debts.
* The number of steps in a stair should be odd such as 3, 5, 7, 9 ...
* Comfortable, attractive and sturdy staircase reflects good vaastu.
* One should never delay repair of broken staircase as this constitutes a serious dosha.
* Spiral staircase is not recommended.
* One can have a storeroom beneath the stairs but never a bathroom, prayer room or a kitchen.
* The steps of a stair should be 10 to 12 inches wide and 7 inches high so that persons of all age groups can move on it comfortably.
* The width of steps in commercial buildings can be between 12 and 15 inches.

If the staircase in one's house do not meet the vaastu requirements and have a related defect, the following remedial measures are adopted to reduce the negative effects:

1. Keeping potted plants on both sides of the steps.
2. If it becomes absolutely necessary to build stairs in the north-east direction then one must go for a wooden staircase as such stairs do not become an integral part of the building and thus do not create dosha.
3. If one lives in a house having a staircase in the northeast and it is not possible to shift it, one must construct a room in the south-west portion of the house and keep its roof higher than the existing staircase.

Storeroom

Every house needs a storeroom and the recommended direction for this is the northwest.

In case northwest is not possible, one may consider building it in south, southwest or west.

In multi-storeyed buildings, a storeroom is recommended on the ground floor only. A storeroom on mezzanine floor can be built in south or west direction.

The door of a storeroom should have two shutters and the doors of a domestic storeroom should not be in the south-west direction.

The window and ventilator should be on east or west wall.

Use the suggested directions for storing the following items in a storeroom:

Grains: These can be stored in the northwest direction.

Dairy products: Items like milk, butter, ghee and cooking oil should be stored in the southeast.

Bulky items: These should be stored in the southwest.

The negative effects of existing Vaastu doshas in a storeroom can be removed by:

1. Using blue or green colour for painting the walls.
2. Using heavy and dark colour material for curtains.
3. Drawing grains or any other eatables from the storeroom only during day time and never at night.

Study Room

If a separate room for study purpose is desired then according to vaastu it is best located in the west direction. A study room in the south-west and north-west is not considered good.

The door of the study room should be in north, north-east or east. A door in the south-east, north-west or south-west is not considered auspicious. Windows should be in the north, east or west side.

Book racks should be placed in the north or east directions but never in south-west or north-west directions. Books placed in the south-west or north-west directions either get lost or stolen or become useless.

Toilet

North-west is the best recommended direction for a toilet but if necessary one can also consider the south-east. A toilet is never permissible in the north-east, south-west and the *brahmasthan*.

A toilet in the north-east can cause financial loss and lack of prosperity for the owner. A toilet in the south-west causes ill health and mental confusion.

A toilet next to a kitchen or worship room is unthinkable.

In order to minimise any negative effects due to Vaastu doshas one should have the walls painted in light colours or use light coloured tiles.

Veranda

Veranda is also spelled as verandah. It is a roofed area with open front at the ground level leading to the main structure of the house. Vaastu recommends a veranda in the north, north-east or east direction as shown in the sketch below. A veranda in the south or west side is never recommended in vaastu as gossiping or loud talking in these directions causes financial loss. The corners of the veranda should be at right angles and not round in shape.

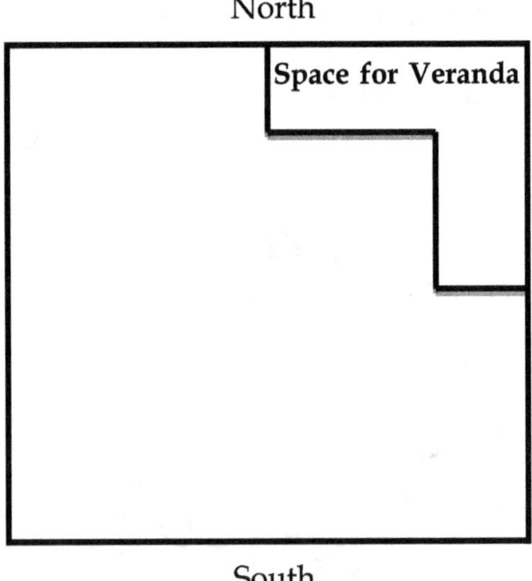

Fig. C 42.1: Sketch showing the Vaastu recommended area where a veranda can be located.

The roof level should be lower than that of the rest of the house.

Common vaastu doshas (defects) and suggested remedial measures

If there is a vaastu defect in a house due to wrong location of a veranda then its negative effects can be minimised by:

1. Hanging a mirror on the wall on the north or east side of the veranda.
2. Placing the shoe rack, if and when required, in the northwest.
3. Placing the required item(s) of furniture in the west or south direction.
4. Making a window on the wall on the north or east side.